Dieuwke Wendelaar Bonga

Eight Prison Camps

A Dutch Family in Japanese Java

Ohio University Center for International Studies
Monographs in International Studies
Southeast Asia Series, Number 98
Athens

© 1996 by the
Center for International Studies
Ohio University
Printed in the United States of America
All rights reserved
02 01 00 99 98 97   5 4 3 2

The books in the Center for International Studies Monograph Series
are printed on acid-free paper ∞

Library of Congress Cataloging-in-Publication Data available

ISBN 0-89680-191-8

*The map of Java showing the location of internment camps during World War II is based on
a map in* De Japanse Interneringskampen voor Burgers gedurende de Tweede
Wereldoorlog *by Dr. D. van Velden published by Uitgeverij T. Wever B.V., Franeker.*

Cover and text designed by Chiquita Babb

Eight Prison Camps

This series of publications on Africa, Latin America, and Southeast Asia is designed to present significant research, translation, and opinion to area specialists and to a wide community of persons interested in world affairs. The editor seeks manuscripts of quality on any subject and can generally make a decision regarding publication within three months of receipt of the original work. Production methods generally permit a work to appear within one year of acceptance. The editor works closely with authors to produce a high quality book. The series appears in a paperback format and is distributed worldwide. For more information, contact the executive editor at Ohio University Press, Scott Quadrangle, University Terrace, Athens, Ohio 45701.

Executive editor: Gillian Berchowitz
AREA CONSULTANTS
Africa: Diane Ciekawy
Latin America: Thomas Walker
Southeast Asia: James L. Cobban

The Monographs in International Studies series is published for the Center for International Studies by the Ohio University Press. The views expressed in individual monographs are those of the authors and should not be considered to represent the policies or beliefs of the Center for International Studies, the Ohio University Press, or Ohio University.

To Liz, Rose, and Lita,
who are my daughters and my friends

Contents

Illustrations

Preface

THIS BOOK is about the ordeal which I, my family, and indeed all Dutch citizens underwent during the Second World War while held prisoner in concentration camps by the Japanese during their occupation of what was then known as the Netherlands East Indies in Southeast Asia. You'll wonder why, after so many years, I want to write about this story of misery and sorrow. Well, there are many reasons, too many to absorb. My main three reasons are as follows:

Number one is that upon our return to the Netherlands from Indonesia in 1946, not many there understood our stories. Their attitude was, "You are making this up, aren't you?" They too had come through the German occupation and the country was recovering from that period. Most folks did not know anything about the war in the Far East and few had time to get involved with more stressed-out people and their problems.

Second, I regard my story as history. Only survivors of war, like myself, can give a personal account of what we went through. Many others remained victims of their memories for the rest of their lives. Also, once my generation passes on there will be no one else who can reveal the firsthand truth about the terrible years in the concentration camps.

And third, my daughters have urged me to write about my experiences. They feel that I have held back too long.

When they were young I told them how I came to grow up in the East Indies, and some camp incidents, but now that they are adults they will be able to cope with the entire story, the horror, the humor, the high points and the low ones. Also, now that I am retired, I seem to ponder more and more about my lost adolescence.

I hope that these memories will make clear the extreme terror, fear, suffering, and humiliation inflicted upon all the men, women, and children in the Japanese prison camps in Southeast Asia and the impact that time has had on their remaining years.

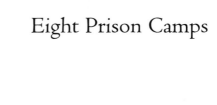

Eight Prison Camps

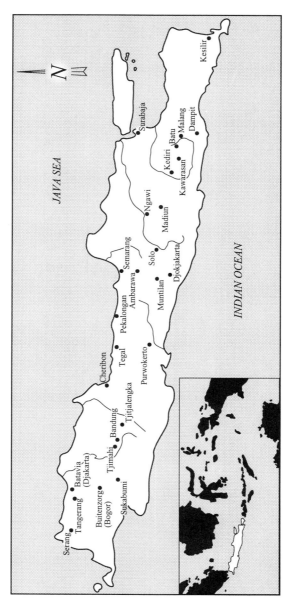

Map of Java showing location of internment camps
during World War II

One

Fore-Fathers and Mothers

My Papa came into this world as the fifth and youngest child of some very hard working parents. His father, Sietse Talsma, was a transporter of milk in Friesland, The Netherlands. He lived on the river Ee, stepped in his row boat (instead of a car) very early in the morning and rowed away from home to pick up the full cans of milk from the farmers. He delivered them to the dairy factory in his hometown Dokkum. This was his life's work. As far as I can remember, Pake (the Frisian name for grandpa) was a small man, friendly, strong-looking, with a weather-beaten face, who did not say much.

Papa's mother's maiden name was Emkje Postma. She was the kindest sweet-smiling Beppe (the Frisian name for grandma) I recall. Papa just adored her. She was quite a tall woman; I suppose Papa got his height from her. I met Pake and Beppe only once, when I was nine years old.

Papa, whose Christian name was Lolke, had two brothers and two sisters. While growing up, all the children started working as soon as they finished public school, but my Papa had other ideas. He wanted to study and become a teacher. This was quite a decision. In the early days of the twentieth century every child had to earn his keep as soon as he could. His mother approved of his plans; his dad did not say much at first, but when Papa turned out to be a good, persistent student he supported him wholeheartedly. The older brothers, however, had some trouble accepting their "baby brother's" easy life.

His persistence showed at one time when on the spur of the moment, Papa as a nine-year old joined a speed skating race, held on the canal in the center of town during a winter festival. The first prize was a pair of skates with real steel blades! Only the rich could afford those skates. Little Lolke skated on his wooden blades. When Papa lined up with all the other little boys he had one aim in mind and . . . he won!

My Beppe said she had never seen her son happier than when he came home with his brand new pair of skates. The church people stood on the doorstep that same night to accuse the boy of participating in "games of chance," which was a great sin! My Pake sent them out of the house with the words, "We have never in our lives seen our boy so happy. This cannot be wrong, he earned those skates. You can go now!" They went with their tails between their legs.

Papa studied hard and later became a teacher. He got to know Mama when he was in teachers college, but she was not a student there. Mama's name was Elizabeth. She was two years younger than Papa and she was the youngest of two daughters of Ids Jousma, who worked all his life for the same boss, the owner of a hardware warehouse. It was heavy work, shipping and receiving tools and iron works. Opa (Grandpa) was a handsome man, stubborn in his ways but with a good sense of humor. Mama told me often how poor they were. Her dad came home with a weekly salary of two and a half guilders, which a family of four had to live on. The family moved to The Hague for a year when Mama was about eight years old and returned to Dokkum because city living was much more expensive and the promised extra money vanished there. They had missed family and friends too much anyway and were not sorry to have come back. Besides, if they had not returned she never would have met Papa!

My grandma, Dieuwke[1] Van de Wal (I am her name-sake) was kind of chubby, and spotlessly clean in caring for herself, her family, and her house. I guess such a trait must be in the genes as most of her offspring have the same "water and soap scrub urge." "Grootmoe" (same as oma, grandma, in Dutch) became severely deaf before she reached middle age. It was hard to converse with her. She was tough though, and lived to the ripe old age of 97.

Mama was called Lies for short and her sister's name was Anna. Mama stayed small while her sister grew to be quite tall. Anna married a baker and stayed in Dokkum all her life. Mama also started working after public school. She became a nanny for a rich family in town. The money she earned was handed over to her parents. Still, she grew up to be a very contented girl. She was a teenager during the First World War, in which Holland stayed neutral.

The economy in Holland was very poor when Papa and Mama became engaged. She was eighteen and he twenty. Papa did not find a teaching position right away. These were hard times for many people and Papa sometimes worked for nothing just to gain some experience. When finally, after

---

1. In Dutch, the name *Dieuwke* is often shortened to *Joke* (much like Jeffrey may be shortened to Jeff in English). I am usually called by *Joke* (pronounced *Yo-ka*), and that is how my name is written throughout the book.

two years, he was called to teach in a small fishermen's village in a one-man school, there was also a house available! How lucky they felt! They married but lived for a while in a barely furnished house as they did not have a cent and could not buy a thing. My brother Sietse was their first-born and not very much later here was I, named after Grootmoe.

They moved to the north of the province of Groningen to another village, where Papa accepted a slightly better paid position. There Emmy was born. With three children expenses rise and, although they were happy in that place, Papa started looking around for a better paid job. He inquired about teaching positions with the Christian Native Schools in the Netherlands East Indies, which had always been of great interest to him while he was studying. But the family objected; in those days you just did not leave and disappear. The Indies were alive and progressing. The job offers were very attractive and Papa applied, not telling his parents!

It was, of course, a great shock to the relatives when they heard the decision of the young family to move to the Indies, the Far East, called poetically, "De Gordel van Smaragd" (the Emerald Belt). But, in 1928 Papa and Mama with three children boarded a big ocean steamer called the *P.C. Hooft* and their big adventure started. The trip lasted four long weeks on board this huge ship, during which they took in a host of new experiences. There was the entertainment, the meals, the cabins, the sunsets, the various oceans and new countries. How impressive it must have been for a young couple who had never traveled before. I cannot remember this trip but I can imagine how much courage it took for Papa and Mama to leave hearth and homeland and glide into the unknown.

Eight Prison Camps

Two

The Indies, Why We Were There

JUST IMAGINE Java, the main island of the Netherlands East Indies in the late 1920s. For someone who has never been in the Far East it is important to understand how different tropical lifestyles are from European or Western ways of living. They didn't know what to expect as they were heading for Surakarta (Solo) in Central Java, which at that time was still ruled by a *sunan* (sultan) and a *mangku* (nobleman).

Papa and Mama soon found out. They arrived from their safe little village in the north of the Netherlands and ventured out to this evergreen country. A family with three children: Sietse, at four years of age, was a redhead. I myself, at three, very, very blond and blue eyed, and Emmy at one, also very fair.

As a teacher, Papa was full of ambitions. But he had always ached to do something more than just teach. Papa's idea of teaching was more than bringing the three "R's" into the schools. Educating the children of this land would give them the chance of self-worth, the possibilities for a better life and the realization that they possessed the willpower to make something of themselves. That was Papa's deeper sense of teaching. He wanted to help educate the population of this wonderful land and had studied everything possible to enrich his knowledge about it before he took the big step of moving there.

One can only understand the feeling of the tropics once one is there. The "Emerald Belt" is actually what the name implies: a wide circle of beautiful evergreen islands, large and small, shining in a glittering hot sun. The equator runs right through Southeast Asia so that the climate is dominated by monsoons—six months of wet weather, six months of dry weather. The three months leading up to the wet weather were very humid and clammy, until the rains began to fall. After this wet season three months of a gradual letting up of the rains would follow, leading into the dry season.

Imagine, no snow, no ice, just a white-hot sun that reigns over this archipelago. Quite a change for young parents to start a new future with three small children. This was also a brave undertaking as they had never been away from their homeland.

Mama and Papa had to get used to a lot of new things. In the first place, there was the "sleeping under *klambues,*" mosquito netting, as mosquitoes were a constant threat in the spread of different kinds of malaria. There was also the threat of dysentery, typhoid, cholera and pest, all very infectious ailments. And although the government had instituted regular inoculation programs, which were free for the whole population and all the school children, the threat was always there!

Their immediate attention was focused on different strange animals and reptiles. Little "tjit-tjaks," wall salamanders, were clinging to the walls of their living room feeding on hundreds of mosquitoes. And then there were the snakes which would slither up their front verandah when the rains came. These snakes were usually the poisonous kind. Mama would pour boiling water on them while we kids were standing right behind her watching.

Then there were the unexpected tropical sounds of crickets, birds shrieking, and of the *tokeh* (large frog-like salamanders). They were real signs of hot humid weather during the wet season.

One acclimatizes after a certain period of time and is able to stand this kind of living. It becomes a delight not to have to cope with fall and winter. A delight to walk out of the house without coats, jackets, or boots, to go biking, swimming, or sporting without freezing to death.

Papa and Mama discovered the splendid mountains and volcanoes with their scenic array of foothills, all covered with dense jungle growth. It would take their breath away. With immeasurably deep ravines and high waterfalls, nature in Java is so green, so inviting, so unforgettable.

Java provides another unsurpassed image in its plant world. Swaying palm trees, coconuts clumped together high on the coconut trees, bougainvillea vines growing over home patios throwing a blessed shade on the hottest days, hedges of blooming *kembang spatu* (hibiscus) showing their hot colors along roads and driveways.

Java is also a country of plantations where sugar cane grew, rubber was produced, and tobacco fields flourished, from which all sorts of products were manufactured. The coffee and tea plantations were mostly on the mountain slopes and a lot of people found work there.

This land had its own exotic fruits, unbelievably good and different and plentiful. We learned to eat and like fruits such as sawoh, bananas, papaya, rambutan, kedondong and djeruk and the list goes on. In our own yard grew mango and djambu trees.

The views of the paddi (rice) fields give the island its exclusive image. Rice, with all its possibilities, is grown here as a national food and is also exported. Still, at the time when Papa and Mama arrived, it was hard to believe that so much poverty existed among the dense overpopulation.

The Dutch government had from the beginning of the twentieth century worked towards the development and education of the vast population. At first it went slowly. This multitude did not seem to understand the purpose of this decision. A laborer did not work hard. He did not plan much for the future. A plate of rice and ten cents a day seemed sufficient, but it was not. Women and children mostly worked in the paddi fields. By the age of thirty they were old and worn out. Papa felt that they should have more to look forward to. He was concerned about their way of living. Gradually things changed, mainly through education and this was Papa's field. He had dreamed about this work when growing up and now he could fulfill his dreams.

Papa and Mama settled in Solo in a large East Indian house. Trying to get used to the climate and the start of Papa's school work took all their time. The first years Papa bicycled to the Idenburg school wearing his white tropical suits and straw dress hat. First he taught grades six and seven and in later years he became the principal of this large native school. On top of all the new impressions he started the study of the Javanese language which would be important to him for the rest of his tropical years.

Mama made new friends who helped her with the hiring of some servants. These native women and girls were always happy to work for the *blandas,* white people, meaning Europeans. She hired a *babu* for the housework, a *kokki* for the preparation of meals, and a young garden boy, a *kebon,* for the rough work around the house. These servants lived in a *kampong,* a native section of town, and would come in for the day. For the three children she found a nanny named Jo, who was not a native, but an Indo girl. Indos are the offspring of usually a Dutch father and native mother, sometimes the other way around. Jo lived in for a while. This worked out very well.

Why so many servants one might ask? Well, when a European arrives in the tropics, he has a real battle with the climate. It takes everything out of him. The lifestyle is almost the exact opposite from the European way. It really is a necessity to have help in order to get accustomed to the heat.

For example, the days start very early, when it is coolest. At six o'clock it is sun-up. Everyone rises, freshens up, has breakfast, and school and work starts at 7:00 or 7:30. Schools run to 12:00 or 12:30 P.M. with sometimes two recess periods. Most people are home again by 1:00 P.M. when dinner is served.

Between 2:00 and 4:00 it is siesta time, when practically the whole country is down and out. Rest, sleep, quiet time, everyone needs this. After 3:30 or 4:00 the *mandi*-room, bathroom, becomes the favored spot in the house.

To *mandi* is a special ritual in the tropics. You soap yourself and then splash cold water over your body with a half-gallon bucket. The water is scooped up out of a cement tile basin of approximately three by three by three feet, built in a corner of the bathroom. The wasted water just runs off into a drain in the floor. It is a different and quite a refreshing, invigorating daily routine. We had a shower too, but the water was always lukewarm.

Mama remembered a newcomer who for the first time went to the *mandi*-room and climbed right into the squared-off basin and sat in it. Later on, among some friends, he declared that he found it rather uncomfortable. Amid hilarious laughter he was told how he was supposed to take a bath in the tropics.

Around 4:00 tea was served and on less hot days we went for walks in the villa park or did some shopping. When we children were growing up we used to have a permanent membership in the town's swimming pool where we spent a lot of our free time with our friends. We had to be home again by 5:00.

Six o'clock was supper and darkness. There is no dawn or dusk in the tropics. Within ten minutes it is dark. Homework after supper for the older ones and bedtime for the little ones, on a normal day. These routines were pretty well kept by most Europeans to deal with the heat.

It was a happy life. As soon as Papa and Mama established their circle of friends and found the church they belonged to, they realized that this was the kind of future they had wished for, for themselves and their children.

Three

The Indies, Our Home

PAPA WAS a tall man, a good six foot three inches, blond with big blue eyes, with which he could direct his pupils and us kids without a lot of fuss. He was a good dedicated teacher who thrived in the Indies. Some of his self-imposed duties were to look up the Javanese problem children of his school in the *kampongs*. Sometimes he had a hard time to persuade the parents to postpone child marriages in order to let the child continue his or her education and he often won! The native families respected him and the children attended school happily.

Mama was small with dark brown hair and she had dark blue eyes. She had taken care of children since she was a young girl and she loved them. She was a born housekeeper and mother. We were not so very long in Solo when my sister Ann was born. I still see Mama coming home with the new baby in her arms. Here in Solo she had to go to the hospital for the delivery and she loved it. Her first three had been born at home in Holland and she always said, "That was very nice, but a lot of work!"

Soon after Sietse and I started school Papa and Mama decided to move from our first house on Wiskalan closer to the villa park. It was actually too far and too hot for us little children to walk to school. Over all, it turned out to be good judgment as we were now closer to church, hospital, swimming pool, and our friends.

Every family had its ups and downs; so did ours but generally we were a healthy bunch. I guess that's why brother Ids made his entrance in the "yellow house," so called because of all the yellow paint. Ids was born in 1931, a boy! After three girls, Papa and Mama were excited. I know they loved us all, but to them it must have been delightful to have another son. He turned out to be my favorite brother.

Liesje came in 1933, a sweet, strawberry blond baby; that was number six. Nowadays we would be called a large family, but Papa and Mama could handle it. We were all good students, were active in sports, and had a lot of friends, an important part of growing up.

By 1934, after six years, Papa was entitled to a furlough in the mother country. So we sold practically everything we owned by means of an auction company. We held on to the beds though and stored them. Then we packed up, found temporary employment for some of the servants, who had become quite close to us, and then we left by passenger ship, the *Sibajak*, for Holland.

Now, I don't want to go into that trip although I remember quite a bit about it. At any rate, it was a good visit. After ten months we were back in Solo in July, 1935. We moved into a large villa in the Villa Park on Margojudan 256. We stayed there until the war broke out in 1942.

I remember this house best. It was bungalow style. It had a large centered front verandah with a long living room.

The dining room was right behind it. On either side of the center rooms were five bedrooms, one of which was a double master bedroom. Papa used one bedroom in the front alongside the verandah as a study. The rooms all had three-meter high walls and ceramic tile floors, which kept the house nice and cool. The windows were big but we had double shutters before them, no glass. We also had double front and back doors with heavy locks, because of thieves. Above the doors and some windows were oval or triangular-shaped openings for ventilation, with decorative ironwork covering the holes. I still consider this house my childhood home.

In the tropics the kitchen, *gudangs* (storerooms), washing facilities, bathrooms and toilet are usually behind the main house. Covered but open galleries, called *empers*, run alongside these rooms. We also had a large garage at the side of the house near the back. It was a big house indeed. It was not our own, we rented it from a family who lived behind us. The rents were low and Papa and Mama took care of repairs or painting if necessary. There was a roomy yard around the house and we had a circular driveway with gravel on it. Fruit and palm trees were nicely set around the house and Mama always had big pots with different tropical plants sitting on the steps around the front verandah. We had a small patio near the front side entrance of that verandah. On the whole, most houses were built of brick or were stuccoed and all in a similar style, cool and comfortable.

I was ten years old when we returned from our overseas voyage. We always attended a Christian school in our city called the Christian European School, though children from all races and nationalities could attend. The school boards of all the Christian schools in the Indies were based in Holland. *All* schools, no matter what religion, were supported by the Dutch government. A lot of our friends lived in the neighborhood and a large group used to walk up together to school. When we were in high school, we rode our bikes. There were several different high schools in our town, which provided excellent education. We grew up among Chinese, Javanese, Arabs, and Indos, as well as people from other backgrounds. For example, in my last high school class there were only three Dutch girls and four Dutch boys, the others were from other nationalities. But among us all, we were friends; we studied together, we had gym together, and we celebrated Christmas together.

What I specifically want to point out about our Christian schools is the singing. I was brought up and always participated in junior and senior choirs in public school. Our Christmas performances were held in the church and were highly praised. Our principal composed most of the songs and he was also the choir director. I sang with my family and my sisters whenever I had a chance. Also at home, every night after supper our whole family sang together, either a hymn, a psalm, or a Dutch folk song. Our servants used to enjoy listening to us and would comment, "*Bagus, bagus*" (nice, nice). Maybe that is one reason why we were relatively happy and optimistic about the future.

Several people have questioned me about the development of cities, towns, and villages in the Indies. I can honestly say that everything was well advanced, even quite modern. The villas and houses were comfortable. We ourselves had good furniture made of the beautiful Javanese *djati hout,* which compares to teak wood, and had carpets on the floor. Every week these carpets were aired in the hot sun to prevent bugs from finding a home in them, which is a serious problem in the Indies. Every day the floors were washed with a disinfectant. This was really a necessity as infections and germs grow rapidly in the steamy heat. We were allowed to walk on our bare feet at home but not on the street. Streets were paved, there were service stations, and there was regular garbage collection. We had electricity and running water. We children all owned bikes. Downtown were long streets with large department stores, also quite a few Japanese stores, shoe stores, and grocery stores. But most of the fresh produce and meats could be bought in the *passar* by means of *tawar* (bargaining). Our *kokki*, named Atmo, would pick up what we needed early in the morning before she would come in to work. Under the skillful money management of Mama, she did very well. Quite a few salespeople also came to the door with materials for sewing, beautiful silks and shantungs and cottons. Mama sewed quite a bit herself and we girls learned early. Also flower salesmen and bakery men were regulars and it was very interesting to go through their wares, which were proudly displayed.

Not only the *blandas* lived in comfortable houses. The native teachers of Papa's school also enjoyed similar luxuries. Papa had a good income but we had a large family with many needs. Papa and Mama were very thrifty and managed their money well. We had a very happy childhood thanks to our loving parents.

To our delight my little brother Peter was born in October, 1938. We sewed, embroidered and knitted in preparation for his arrival. He became the center point in our family. Papa and Mama were like a young couple again. We all loved that little boy.

When little Pete was almost ten months old, Sietse left us to continue his education in Holland. He finished high school at fifteen and the nearest university or college was in

Bandung in west Java. Sietse's intended technical courses were not available over there. Papa had contacted a good friend in Holland who arranged for room and board for Sietse in Leeuwarden in the province of Friesland. Quite a few families had children in the same age group. Some mothers decided to return with all their children while the fathers remained behind, maybe for only a year or so, until retirement or furlough. Sietse could travel with them, by train and ship. He seemed very independent when he parted from us, but I guess he must have missed us. Several of his best friends traveled with him, which probably helped. For Mama and Papa it was hard to see their first-born leave home and go so far away.

From then on I became the oldest at home, which was quite a realization for me. I had started the same high school as Sietse the year before he left. After finishing the first year there, I could switch over to a newly opened school, the H.B.S. (Higher Citizen School), which was very popular in Holland. Several of my girlfriends had left for Holland and the remaining one stayed in the other high school. But I managed and enjoyed the new school and my new friends very much.

In August, 1940, our family got another surprise with the arrival of my youngest sister Elly. Of course we knew that Mama was expecting again. And when the baby arrived, she was beautiful. Very fair and with big blue eyes. She was number eight for Mama and Papa but to us all she was number one. She had, like little Pete, five mothers, four sisters and Mama, plus a little native nursemaid Sujatih.

We doted on the little ones. They took away some of the worry and anxiety of the war in Europe, where Holland also had fallen to the Germans in May of the same year.

Mama and Papa worried so much about Sietse. His letters and the family's stopped coming. The radio told about the bombings and the parachutists taking over the country, but we could not do a thing about it.

Several fathers, whose families had returned to Holland when Sietse left in 1939, still tried to get away to join and support their loved ones. Some made it, some could not get through any more. It was a hopeless feeling for them. Still, where we were nothing changed and life continued in the same routines.

Our living conditions changed somewhat when Mama acquired an electric stove and refrigerator, which really improved the kitchen facilities. And Papa had bought his first car, a large, square seven-seat Fiat. Instead of going on vacation to the mountain resort Tawangmangoe by bus, as we used to do, we could now take our own car. This resort was closest to Solo on the slopes of the mountain Lawu. We rented a cottage for the long holidays in July and used to come back all rosy-cheeked and refreshed for the upcoming year. In 1940 Papa changed the Fiat for a 1939 Chevy and we had also changed from Tawangmangoe to a resort in Kopeng, above Salatiga on the mountain Sumbing, still in central Java. It was a bit farther away but the roads were not as steep. Now that we could go more often, Papa and Mama decided to have their own cottage built near Ngablak, just past Kopeng. It was very beautiful there, more remote and quiet.

A well known Chinese carpenter was hired to build the furniture for the cottage, which was first stored in our *gudangs* and some cabinets were placed in our bedrooms, where we could use them until the cottage was ready.

Our mountain trips bring back very special memories

to me. Nature in the mountains was so green and impenetrable. The air was so fresh and clear. Sleeping under a blanket was an adventure. We did not need that in the valley of the *kali* (river) Solo. We climbed steep foothills, small mountains in themselves. At one time we climbed up a dry ravine as far as we could go. That was such a wild and fierce trip, all rock and jungle around us. Unforgettable!

Once Mama stayed longer up at a cottage we had rented. School had started again for us children. When after a few weeks she came home she surprised us all with an adorable little white mixed-breed Pekinese puppy. The cottage owner's dog had had a litter and she had picked this one. We were crazy about the little pet. We already had a lovable mutt named Fanny besides our cats, pigeons, and ducks. I particularly was delighted as I usually took care of our menagerie. Little Molly could not have picked a better home.

Our life went on normally. School, girlfriends, boyfriends, swimming, tennis, biking and taking turns looking after the little ones. As children we were not too concerned about the war. Of course, the new baby Elly filled our lives with so much pleasure. Both Peter and Elly were the center of our family life.

But even if we older girls were not too upset about the war in Europe, we were nonetheless conscious of it. The adults were always talking about it and there were so many rumors about it, one hardly knew what to believe.

When little Elly had her first birthday in August, 1941, there were a lot of rumblings between the United States and Japan, and Japan and China (Manchuria), and Russia and Germany and Japan. But we thought nothing of it. It was so far away from us. We prayed for Holland's freedom, we hoped for word from Sietse and that was all we could do.

And I, as a sixteen-year-old, had to write my exams, and I went swimming and played tennis with Emmy and our friends. Where was the war?

Four

The Unexpected Arrives

The threat of war came closer. Even after the shocking attack on Pearl Harbor on December 7, 1941, by Japan, our faith in our own military, navy and airforce was wholehearted. We did not expect anything serious would happen to us. The news on the radio was not encouraging but we carried on as usual.

Mind you, there was no T.V., so we did not see anything of the terrible damage of the assault on Hawaii. Our schools were on, we swam every day and we were looking forward to our Christmas concert.

However, from the 7th of December on, things went downhill. Our ears were glued to the radio. The next day already the Japanese attacked two airfields in the Philippines, Clark and Iba. Landings were made and heavy fighting was going on. In the meantime, strikes followed on Malaya and the oil regions of the British and Dutch Balikpapan and Tarakan. It was full war in that area of Asia.

Just after Christmas, on December 27, Manilla in the Philippines was being bombed, even after it was declared an open city (open cities are not supposed to be bombed!).

By the end of that year, within a month of the attack on Pearl Harbor, we were not so sure any more about this attacking force that seemed so organized. Papa and Mama decided to have a bomb shelter built in the very back of our yard, just in case of air raids. We questioned our parents about the seriousness of this action, it all seemed so far off. "The possibility is always there," said Mama, "and we are with so many, we should do it."

Evacuees started to arrive from the islands around us. Bertha Harwig, a friend of ours, came to stay with us from Timor with her little two-year-old boy. We had been friends with the Harwigs since Bertha and her husband, Joe, a soldier with the K.N.I.L. (Royal Netherlands Indian Army), were married in our home. Papa also used to work a lot with the lonely soldiers and Joe had been a regular visitor at our house. Bertha was pregnant again and for safety sake all the women and children had been advised to draw back to Java. She never saw her dear husband again. We heard later that he had died from an infectious illness while he was still in Kupang, on the island of Timor.

Now there were eleven persons at home and the outlook was not encouraging. Every citizen was advised by radio and newspaper how and what to prepare for emergencies, where to hide in case of air attacks, what to pack if your home had to be evacuated.

Mama's seamstress sewed a backpack for each of us older ones and we discussed together what the contents should be. Mama also packed a couple of suitcases with clothes for the little ones, Peter and Elly, with clothes for "growth." "We never know what can happen," she said, "The children outgrow their clothes so fast. I have to have some for the future." She also packed some rations like canned meat, dried milk powder, and some packages with arrowroot biscuits.

Furthermore, every person who owned a car had to deliver it to certain checkpoints for emergency purposes. Our car had to go also. Then Papa decided to offer his services as a volunteer in the army. We did not like to see Papa go, but several other teachers left with him and they were placed in Malang in East Java. We heard from him occasionally and he said it was not too bad among the "boys."

We children still went to school for a while but more and more teachers were called up for duty or they went to get trained as replacement staff in hospitals or as Red Cross workers. I was in the third year of high school now. Most classes were held part-time, other schools were completely closed. That meant that there were eight children, Bertha's little Johnny included, home all day. We older ones realized that this was very different but actually, nothing happened.

We were just in the first weeks of January, 1942, when Emmy and I, as teenagers, were approached to help out at an air control service. That meant shift work during the night from 9:00 P.M. to 3:00 A.M. or from midnight to 6:00 A.M. Our job was to take telephone messages and record reports from different observation posts around our city about enemy aircraft sightings.

It was an easy job and, we felt, a fun part of our war volunteering. Emmy, I, and Els, a girlfriend of mine who lived close to us, were picked up by the Muiden's private car. The Muiden's daughter, Petra, who was in the same high school class with me, was also in our group. Her parents became our trainers and guardians. There were eight girls, one mother included. The other staff members were older officers who took action on our messages.

The air control service checkpoint was kept in a bunker-type building of solid concrete, buried about three-quarters underground. It was strong, in case of air raids, but we thought nothing of it. We had time to chat, play cards, we just had to be there.

The first weeks were rather dull. Nothing happened except for the fun we had. We even designed a khaki uniform dress. Mama, with the help of our seamstress, had the dresses ready in no time. We felt important to be working for our country. Later, in February, when mysterious codes were reported from the lookout posts, which put the whole staff of officers in frantic action, we felt deeply that the fun was over, that there was more to war than having a good time!

On the 15th of February, 1942, Singapore fell to the Japanese. Thousands and thousands were slaughtered. There were hardly any more men around in our town but I cannot remember that we were worried. But the closer it drew to the end of the month the more depressing the news became. Mama was very anxious when Emmy and I left for night duty. She often said, "I wish you could stay home. It makes me sick, you are just children!" which upset us, for at that time we were really needed and were doing important work. I don't know if it was Mama's intuition, because not very long afterwards we girls were told not to come any more. No reason was given, but we understood!

By the end of the month our streets were suddenly wild with jeeps, trucks, and fight wagons crowded with retreating troops—our troops, which were Dutch, British, Australian, and some Americans. There had been great losses at sea we heard, and the onslaught was frightening. When there was a slowdown in the long uninterrupted chain of vehicles we talked to the men and gave them drinks. They looked tired and worried, but on they moved. In the meantime, behind our house near the *kali* Solo, the B.P.M. (Batavia Oil Company) oil reservoirs burnt. We could hear the roaring of the fire and could see the flames high up in the sky. It was scary.

The Japs had actually landed in three places on Java on February 28. Masses of storm troops had been thrown ashore. They moved on folding bicycles. Rumors of rapings and immense cruelties were circulating. The news on the radio revealed that a lot of these troops were Korean life-prisoners who could fight themselves to freedom, that they were desperate! It sure made me think!

Then, all of a sudden the streets were empty, no traffic, no people. Our servants did not come in for work. We relied only on the news on the radio. In those last days of February there was not very much to lift our spirits. "Be prepared," was the message and again we heard rumors of retreating troops (which we had seen), also of naval battles in the Java Sea, of Allied cruisers and battleships sunk. Still, it seemed so far away.

In the first week of March we heard strange rumblings in the air which we could not identify. Mama said, "I am sure it is gun fighting!" We older girls were skeptical. What did we know? But then, especially when it was very still, the sounds, like far away rolling thunder, were becoming louder.

One night, that first week in March, when we were all asleep, Papa came home. I heard it. It was very late. There were dragging footsteps on the gravel of the driveway (my bedroom was at the front of the house). I heard his voice calling Mama's name. Then, scuffling in the house, Mama and Bertha at the front door exclaiming greetings, more muffled sounds and talk.

I got up and, seconds later, entered Mama and Papa's bedroom. Papa was lying on the bed with a bandage wrapped around his head. My first impression was that he had been wounded. Mama saw me and told me straight out, "Go back to bed and keep quiet. Don't wake anybody, you can't do anything anyway." I guess she was very nervous.

I went, but not before I learned what was wrong with Papa. Mama whispered, "He said he fell off a truck and he has a head wound and a slight concussion. His sergeant sent him home as it happened in our town."

I stayed awake pretty well all night. There was a lot of whispering talk and running around. Early in the morning, towards dawn, Mama left the house. I heard the front door, then her footsteps on the gravel and I was wondering what was happening. I, as an obedient girl, stayed in bed, but soon I heard her come back. She was not alone. I peeked and saw that the man with her was one of our ministers, the Reverend Kuiper. More talk and scuffling in the house. After a little while, Papa and the minister left together. Mama was crying.

Early that morning when we were all up, Mama told us the whole story: During the retreat of the troops the truck Papa was on had stopped short, Papa had lost his balance, and fell off landing on his head. A medic had bandaged him up but Papa was very dizzy. His sergeant knew that Solo was Papa's hometown and had given him permission to go home. Even if Papa knew our town inside out, it had still been quite a distance to walk and he was not feeling well at all! Even so, he had made it home. He had cried. He felt like he had deserted his troop and did not want to stay. "If only I had a car," he had said, "then I could join them in Jogja-karta." But our car had also been confiscated.

Then Mama had an idea. She had thought of our ministers who had been permitted to keep their cars for special services. One minister lived just around the corner from our street. That's why she had left so early to try this last solution for Papa's escape. Reverend Kuiper had instantly offered his car and had come along to see if he could help. Mama had added a bottle full of gasoline, which she had kept in the *gudang,* to the car's tank just to make sure Papa would make it.

Papa knew all the back roads through his work with the native families of his school. Taking that route he could move faster than the retreating troops and possibly would be able to join them again before the advancing Japanese could block all the main roads and highways. Papa had been so sorry that he could not stay with us but after everything he had heard, he was sure that the Japanese would kill him right in front of his family if he was found at home. That had been another reason why he had been so adamant to leave.

We all listened to Mama and understood. That was a sad day for us all although we also felt relieved. I kept on thinking about Papa all day. Later we heard from a very good native friend of Papa that he had come through and that he had found his battalion!

However, a couple of days later, Java was also in Japanese hands. On March 9, General Ter Poorten, commanding officer of the K.N.I.L. (Dutch Army), capitulated. Over 20,000 Allied troops surrendered, of which 11,300 were Dutch, 5,600 British, 2,800 Australian and 800 American. Most of our troops, Papa and his friends included, had retreated to Bandung in west Java. That's where they were captured and transported to the various prison camps, but we didn't learn about all that until much later.

Five

First Encounter

THAT SAME DAY after Papa had left, we were all quite depressed. None of the servants had come in. Even our live-in *babu*, Sukarmih, had left, so Mama got her own little troops working. We had to make the beds and clean up clothes and do dishes. It just had to be done and it kept us busy.

We felt relatively safe in our big house but the sounds of battle around our town had become louder. There were also continuous faint murmurs in the air. Very strange. We older ones were glad that Papa was *not* with us. It had been weeks now that we had been cooped up at home and the situation had worsened from day to day. We had quite a few provisions in the *gudang*, we were not worried about starving. Still, Mama and Bertha did not smile much and we were all in a certain state of fearful expectation.

Around ten in the morning Mama asked me to let the *kerees* (bamboo roll curtains) down in the front verandah. This large verandah stuck out quite far in front of our house into the front yard, just like a garage. It was surrounded with a decorative wood carved balustrade with entrances on each side. This balustrade was approximately one and a half meters high. When the heat of the tropical sun hit the house, the bamboo shades were let down all around it to keep the house cool. Normally our *kebon* performed this chore, but I did not mind doing it.

Five of the six shades were down. One more to go in the front center and that was it. Then I saw them . . . across the street! I froze, let go of the cord in my hand and ducked behind the balustrade. A group of Japanese soldiers was crawling alongside the bushes of a small wild-park across our street. Bayonets on rifles, dressed in grey-brown battle wear, from underneath their helmets their narrow eyes were focused on the sky. That was my luck. My first impression was, "They have not seen me . . . yet. Don't move!" I stayed flat on the floor of the verandah. I could have been killed right there and then.

After a long minute I slowly backed away towards our double front doors within the verandah, slipped inside and locked them. I ran through the living room to the dining room at the back of the house and whispered excitedly, "They're here, the Japs are here! I saw them just now, in the ditch across the street!" Everyone stood around me while I described them and their weapons. I was scared and so was my family. We kept quiet for the longest time, even the youngest children seemed to sense our fear.

After a while, when nothing happened and nobody seemed to come to the house, we made lunch. The smaller ones asked for something to eat and drink and while we all ate we discussed what to do. Mama said, "I think it is better that we bring all our suitcases and backpacks to the *gudangs* and stay in this area for the time being." We did that and we all stayed on the *empers* at the very back of the house where there were several rooms side by side kept as kitchen, guest room, *gudangs*, washroom, and so forth.

Since I had seen the soldiers we had also noticed that the strange sounds in the air had become louder, sounds of rousing voices humming, of breaking glass or knocking on wood, just noise off and on. But nothing happened and the noise stayed. It frightened us. We were guessing what it could be while it grew later in the day.

Mama was very restless and no wonder. Such a responsibility rested on her shoulders with all of us there. When evening fell, she said, "We cannot stay here tonight. I don't think it is right to go to bed" (our house was big). "If something happens I can't get you all out together. Let's go into the shelter in the backyard."

There we went, with all our backpacks, suitcases, some food and drink and we crawled into this limited space shelter. Bad idea, Mama! We were not even in there five minutes when plans were changed. "Let's go to the neighbors," Mama said. "This place is too small for all of us!"

An Indo family, the Pieters, was our landlord, but also our friend. We were waiting in the yard when Mama came out of their house and told us, "There's nobody home!" Now the sounds in the air and the raised voices, such as screams and yells, had diminished somewhat, but we were scared to go back to our place.

There was a large old shed in the landlord's back yard and the door was unlocked. We moved in there and settled with all our emergency suitcases and everything else on the floor and on a couple of garden chairs. I carried our little dog Mollie. Where our mutt Fanny was, I don't know.

As darkness surrounded us from 6:00 at night on, we

spent a dreadful night in this shed. The heat suffocated us and the mosquitoes devoured us. Not knowing who would discover us, we had to keep very quiet. With so many small children in our family, there were only a few whimpers now and then. Ids said, "Let's pray Mama, I am scared!" I guess we prayed all night as hardly any of us could sleep.

With ten persons in such a small area it proved impossible to stay there for any length of time. As soon as dawn peeked into the darkness we packed up and moved back to our house. It was quiet there and nothing was disrupted. We all needed some washing up and afterwards ate some breakfast. We stayed on the *empers* in the back.

It was still early when suddenly we heard the same odd noises again, but closer now. Then there was loud banging, hammering and knocking. Just as we were looking at each other with fear in our eyes, out of the blue several native men stormed wildly out of our dining room towards us in the back. They were not after us though, they did not harm us. It seemed like they were in a daze and did not even see us. They had some items out of our home in their arms and tried to enter the *gudangs* behind us.

In a flash Mama sprung into action. With baby Elly on her arm, she moved towards the intruders. In a loud voice, speaking in the Malay language, she shouted, "*Tida boleh, tida boleh!*" (you can't do that), "*pigih, pigih,*" (go away) "*itu saja!*" (that is mine), and she actually pushed several out of the way and . . . they left!

But they kept on coming! The front doors had apparently been bashed in. Hundreds of natives roamed through our house taking everything within their reach with them. They took the *klambus* from the beds, dragged mattresses outside, and ransacked all the closets and cabinets. They plucked the curtains off the windows and ran around with dishes and cutlery. They took everything!

Some robbers were very organized. They had crews of men with them who were ordered to take all the furniture. One such a person was the Chinese carpenter who had made the cabinets and other items for our cottage which were stored in our *gudangs*. He stood there with a big smirk on his face and just went in and got it all! Mama shook her head at him to no avail. And I saw one of our former servants with her arms full of nicknacks. She and many others wore white headbands around their heads. To this day I still don't know what that meant.

Mama went inside the main house twice to throw them out, pushing them and at times hitting them with a rubber sheet from the baby's crib. At the same time she was telling them to "get out!" Even Bertha, in her condition, kicked some of them in the pants so that they scurried out of the way.

But there were just too many. We all persuaded Mama to stop. It was hopeless. Everything was gone anyway. She agreed. In all the commotion my little dog Mollie had disappeared. It all happened so fast! I could not find or see him anywhere. But there was no time to worry about him. We did not even have time to be scared. We stuck together and just had to let it come over us. Through all this turmoil the little ones did not even cry. They stayed close to us and with their big blue eyes wide open, they did not understand.

Until, all of a sudden, it happened. A big *rampokker* (robber) ran right into our little group and grabbed one of our largest suitcases out of Emmy's hands and sped off with it into the backyard. Emmy promptly raced after the man, but got stuck in the wash-lines with her backpack. She wriggled herself free but was too late, the man got away! We all called out to her, "Let go Emmy, let it go!"

She was standing there among all those wild-looking people when we saw her being seized by a camouflaged Japanese soldier, who took her by her arm and led her around the right side of our house to the front. Suddenly there were more of them. They shouted and screamed with raw hoarse voices at the *rampokkers* and at us. We did not understand a word of it. They seemed to order us to do something, but what? They must have spoken Japanese but it could have been any language and nobody would have understood it. The yelling was almost as scary as the whole robbery. Mama kept on nodding her head at one of them who seemed to be in charge. To us she whispered, "Stay together, whatever happens, stay together!" What could we do? We could not stay where we were, there was nothing left! Everything was gone, what a mess! And where was Emmy?

The Japanese soldiers by then had started to chase all the plunderers out of the yard, hitting them with the butts of their rifles. Did they ever run. In a way, that was a good feeling! Then they concentrated on us. They roared and yelled a lot, which was very strange to us. We were not used to being yelled at. This was our first encounter with the enemy and they actually got us out of a mess this time, although they scared us to death. But, where was Emmy?

The soldier in charge motioned us to follow him and he led the way by the left side of the house to the front. We picked up our belongings, suitcases, minus the one with all the children's clothes, our backpacks and all, and made it to the street in a hurry. Luckily, there was Emmy, waiting on the road near a couple of cars. The Japs were still hitting *rampokkers* out of the yard. Some lay bleeding on the gravel.

It all went fast. Here we were loaded into a large car. We sat on top of each other but we stayed together, ten persons in the back and a Japanese driver. Another one beside him, in the front with the bayonet on his rifle. All in one car! They drove us to one of their headquarters further down the street near the railway station.

The last thing I noticed as the car drove off was our little nursemaid, Sujatih, standing near our driveway. She was holding my little Pekinese dog Mollie, my baby, on a leash!

Six

Headquarters

THE JAPS had established headquarters all over town. We did not know where we were heading when we were taken away. Well, the car stopped not very far from our house at this colossal Chinese villa. The owner was probably chased out by the enemy as, at first glance, it was crawling with tiny Japanese soldiers. When they wanted something, they took it!

Jeeps stopped, army trucks pulled up. Battle-ready Japs hopped in and out and entered the villa. Officers yelled orders and the whole scene looked like a busy beehive when our car arrived. We practically rolled out of the steaming hot car and were hustled up the wide front steps of the villa into a large open verandah surrounded by a divided carved marble wall.

Quite a few women and children were sitting on the floor. There were also Indo-Dutch families there. Some were later imprisoned with us, others were regarded as natives and set free. Everyone sat on one side of the verandah. We did not know any of them. But on the other side of the verandah sat one man and I recognized him!

"Mama," I whispered when we were looking for a spot to fall down with our little group, "that is Mr. Muiden!" He did not look at us. Mama said, "Are you sure?" "Yes," I said, "but he looks different somehow, so pale and sad."

I knew where he lived, right across the street from the headquarters. Mr. Muiden was the father of my best girl-friend in high school and our guardian and guide at the air control service a month earlier. Petra was the only daughter of the Muidens. Her father was a very nice gentleman and he was a government official. I got to know him pretty well when Petra and I were together visiting each other. He was always jovial and a great father to his daughter.

We all settled on the floor in his area, which was the biggest open space. It seemed that all the other people had found a spot as far away as possible from the man on the floor. I had no idea how long he had been there. Little Peter started to play with some of the other children there and Elly fell asleep on Mama's lap. I was amazed how these little ones had come through the *rampokking* ordeal. Up to now, they had not cried or fussed at all. It was as if they understood that this was an emergency. Peter looked up so trustingly when Mama told him to stay close to us.

I concentrated on the man on the floor. I spoke softly, "Mr. Muiden, is that really you?" He lifted his head slightly and looked at me, "Joke, you're here?"

"Yes," I whispered, "with my whole family. What did they do to you?" "Unbelievable," he mumbled, "don't talk too much to me, they're watching!"

Mama listened to our conversation and asked, "Did they torture you?" He nodded his head. "Out of the middle ages," he mumbled and slumped down again. We all looked horrified at the poor heap of a man on the floor.

I was wondering where his wife and daughter were. As soon as the Japs in the front were not watching I asked him about it and he answered, "I don't know and it makes me sick."

Mama had filled our large thermos with water and ice cubes early in the morning before the trouble started. Luckily we had it with us. She put some ice cubes in a cup, placed it on the floor and with her foot she shoved it towards Mr. Muiden so that it ended up behind his bleeding hand. He saw it and said softly, "Thanks, I had nothing to drink since yesterday." In the tropics it is crucial to take in liquids. After a whole day without a drink, he could easily have been dehydrated. Especially in his condition, it might have been fatal!

He picked up an ice cube and sort of smuggled it up to his mouth. He continued doing this until his cup was empty. Gradually he told us what the Japs had done to him. First they had beaten him severely and kicked one of his knees out of the socket. To attract bugs and mosquitoes, they had poured sugared liquids over him. He was also full of welts and bug bites. All afternoon Mama fed him ice cubes and we could see him pick up his strength. He was so grateful, he kept on whispering, "You are a Godsend, you are a Godsend."

More and more people were brought in. The wife of the minister who lived close to us, Mrs. Kuiper, came in with four small children, including a three-week old baby. She was happy to see us but we could not talk much. Children are children and they have to go to the bathroom. When the little girls had to go, their mother, while holding the baby, said to her older boy, "Klaas, you can take the girls. Go and ask where it is and come back as soon as possible." At that moment, Mr. Muiden turned towards her and spoke softly but firm, "Madame, don't let your children go alone. These are dirty, evil people! Don't leave your kids alone."

Mama and Emmy took care of the baby so that Mrs. Kuiper could go with her children. When the little group came back the baby was crying. Mrs. Kuiper told us quietly that they had also been picked up from their home. She had rushed into the bedroom to pick up the baby out of its crib against the Japs' orders. Luckily she had gotten away with it, but she had not been allowed to bring anything for the baby.

She did not have one diaper with her and worse, no bottles or formula. A pregnant lady with us on the verandah lent her some diapers so that she could change her baby. Mama had a can with dried milk with her and one way or other they fixed a bottle for the baby. It is amazing how inventive people become in times of need.

We heard from one of the women that the Japanese had expected the Dutch houses to be full of soldiers ready for battle. For this reason, they had sent the natives in first to bear the brunt of any surprise attack. This meant that even if the natives had prompted the plundering, the Japs had encouraged them! When their assumption had turned out to be false, they had had a hard time stopping the *rampokkers.*

We stayed all afternoon at the headquarters. The little ones napped on Mama's lap but I cannot remember that they were whiny or troublesome. Mama urged us girls over and over again not to look at the Japanese and to keep one of the children on our lap. Due to the rumors about the behavior of the Japs, Mama was scared for her daughters! That whole day I did not go to the bathroom!

Late in the afternoon, a couple of army trucks pulled up. Some soldiers or guards entered the verandah, ordered us all up on our feet and motioned and shouted at us to follow them. We all had to climb into a truck. We stayed close together, carrying our backpacks on our backs making sure the suitcases were coming along. As soon as everyone was loaded on, off we went. Everyone except Mr. Muiden. We said good-bye to him and wished him the best. He looked very lonely and pale there on the floor. That was the last I ever saw or heard of him.

We were driven to a large public school which was close to our own Christian public school. It all went *"Lekas, lekas, lekas"* (fast, fast, fast). That was the only word the Japanese could sort of pronounce properly and they used it forever and for everything. The ride was definitely reckless, as if the driver purposely wanted to shake us up. Then we were literally dumped at the school. Immediately the trucks sped off again.

The school was already full of women and children and an occasional older man. We discovered a lot of our friends there who also lived in the Villa Park. All of them had been plundered a couple of days before us. And most of them also had nothing left but their life and a backpack on their backs.

Seven

The Public School, Camp I

As soon as the trucks had been unloaded the soldiers left without looking back. We stood there with our emergency luggage, watching this unbelievable scene of hundreds of people walking, sitting, and lying around. A couple of ladies approached us and said hello. They did not ask any questions but only inquired if we were all right. We noticed the principal of our Christian public school, Mr. Van der Pols coming towards us. The ladies had advised us to look around and find a place to stay in one of the classrooms. We greeted Mr. Van der Pols, and he guided us through the classrooms while we exchanged the latest of our experiences.

The school was built in a huge square. Three lines in the square were the classrooms. The fourth line ran along the road and there were the gates. Coming in from the street into the centre of the square were the playgrounds. Rows of shade trees were set all along the open galleries which ran alongside the classrooms. This kind of structure is typical of the tropics. It shades the buildings from the heat but during hot tropical monsoon rains one can still be outside.

As we arrived late in the day, space was only available in some of the classrooms closest to the road. We moved our belongings in there and settled on the floor alongside one of the inner walls.

Mama was very tired and so was Bertha. The previous night nobody had slept in that shed, so they stretched out on the bare floor with a backpack under their heads and tried to rest. We took the little ones outside to explore our surroundings and sure enough, we found quite a few of our friends there. Everybody had been plundered.

We found the toilets (that was a first!), the *mandi*-rooms, and showers. It was a mess in there. There were just too many people. It became worse when some ladies started to wash out some clothes. Everything was overflowing and smelly. Luckily, there *was* running water.

Nobody could go outside the school grounds for food and lots of people had nothing to eat. At that point we did not know what was going to be done about the food situation. The ladies who had welcomed us came by the washrooms to observe the chaos there.

There were children playing in the playgrounds but there were also a lot of children crying. I remember how hot it was. We could do nothing else but return to the room where we were staying.

We told Mama and Bertha what we had seen and how long the line-ups were for the bathrooms. Mama and Bertha went to wash up a bit and when they came back we divided some leftover food. That was our supper. In the meantime it had become dark and the mosquitoes did their best as nobody had *klambus*. Mama prayed with us, realizing the seriousness of our situation. We asked the Lord to guide us in the days to come and also to be with our Papa, as we did not know what had become of him.

Our room had filled up with strangers. Pretty soon we all felt the strain of the events of the long day and we lay down beside each other on the bare floor. As far as I can remember we had no problem sleeping as we were worn out.

Very, very early in the morning people started stirring to get to the washrooms and showers. Before long we stood in the line-ups. When our turn came it was so nice to be able to freshen up and it made us all feel much better. I don't know how we were fed those days but it did not seem important as the whole situation was so unusual, to say the least.

This new morning I was sitting on the steps of the gallery in front of our classroom when two native policemen walked up to the front gate. With them were two women. The policemen opened the gate, let the ladies enter the yard and then left. I saw who they were. It was Petra Muiden and her mother!

As our room was so close to the street, I ran up to them calling, "Petra, Petra, Mrs. Muiden, how are you?" Then I noticed that they were crying and I also noticed how bedraggled and tired and dirty they looked. They hardly reacted to my greetings, but Petra squeezed my hand. I walked up with them and more ladies came up to offer help. It seemed that they were in a confused state. They were taken into one of the rooms on the other side of the schoolyard. I waited for a long time outside this room. I heard someone saying that there was a doctor with them.

Finally Petra came out, she was still crying. She held a towel and soap in her hands and when she saw me, she sobbed harder and asked me if I wanted to come to the *mandi*-room with her. "Of course," I said and while we walked over to the bathrooms, she kept on crying. When she started washing herself with lots and lots of soap, she told me what had happened to her and her mom.

The night before we had arrived at the Japanese head-quarters, two or three Japanese soldiers had come to their house and had, very roughly, taken her dad away. Before she and her mom had a chance to escape or hide, a couple of Japs had come back and had made themselves comfortable in their living room. Petra was ordered to play the piano for them and they had appreciated that very much, to the point that they had started to stroke her face and caress other parts of her body.

Then they had begun to shout and one of them had sent Petra's mom into the backyard with a bayonet in her back. Although he had not hurt her, she had been frightened to death in the pitch dark, fully realizing what was going to happen to her only daughter. She had hidden herself in the farthest corner of the yard. In the meantime, the other Jap had thrown Petra on the bed in one of the bedrooms and had raped her.

"Oh Joke," she cried, "remember how we sometimes giggled and made fun when we talked about sex? Now one of those dirty Japs did it with me!" Again she burst out crying, "I'll never get married. I feel so dirty!" And again she washed and washed. . .

I was stunned and speechless. My best friend in high school! She was so pretty, also witty and smart. With her dark curly hair, fair skin and blue eyes, she was a remarkable girl. No wonder those soldiers had come back, but with such a vicious purpose! I was thinking fast, "If this is the beginning of the invasion, what is awaiting us?"

But I said to her, "Petra, it's not your fault! You did not want it. You are with friends now and for the time being you are safe. But tell me, how in the world did you get out of there?" While I helped her dry herself and get dressed, she continued, "I held myself as stiff as possible, the doctor said that I am not very damaged. Now, as soon as the Jap got off me and left the room, I rolled off the bed and jumped out of the window. That's where these bruises come from," and she showed me her knees, elbows, and hands.

"Then I ran into the backyard. It was so dark and luckily the guy did not come after me. I found mom. We climbed over the dividing wall in the very back and ended up in a *kampong*. Mom and I were devastated and when we ran into a barbed wire fence, we tried to cut our wrists. We did not want to live any longer!"

I reacted, "Oh no, oh no!" But she continued, "We could not do it Joke, it was too painful. We spent the whole night crying in the dark while hiding in the bushes. When it became light, we did not know where we were and there was nobody around. We stayed in the bushes, just too scared we might run into some Japs again. Our second night was horrible. Then some native people discovered us early at dawn. They warned the policemen, who used their emergency first aid for our wrists and walked us to this school. The doctor has examined us and bandaged our wrists with fresh bandages, but Joke, I am so depressed!"

I comforted her as best as I could. It seemed that all my own experiences about the plundering and robbery were diminished. I did not even mention them to her. Instead, I told her about finding her father in the headquarters across from their villa and what we had done for him. She was so happy to hear he was still alive and said, "Oh, I'll tell mom about this, she will be so glad!"

She was so exhausted though that I took her back to her room. I didn't see her and her mom again that day. I guess they rested and slept off their misery. Deep in thought I wandered back to our classroom to tell Mama and Emmy about Petra and her mom. They were just as shocked as I was. It really did something to me. I hated the Japs!

Suddenly, while we were discussing this sad incident, a Japanese soldier wandered into our room from the street. My thoughts went immediately to what had happened to Petra and I guess so were Mama's! There were not many people in the room but the ones who were there at once straightened up and looked at the man. He concentrated his attention on a young woman who was resting on the floor with her small child. She had not realized that he had come in.

Mama whispered to me and Emmy, "I'll stay here with the kids. Try to get out of here and warn the ladies in the main office." As casually as possible we strolled out of there, once outside I ran across the school yard, but apparently other ladies and children had seen him go into the class-room also. About ten ladies entered the room. The more the better, that was something to remember for future occasions.

The aggressive Japanese did not like crowds when sin-gling out women. The head lady of the camp bowed for him and then motioned him with hand gestures to follow her. She tried to ask him if she could do something for him or if he maybe was looking for someone? He stared at all the ladies, then marched out of the room, out of the school-yard, out of the gate and disappeared into the street. Every-body sighed. The woman on the floor was so grateful, "I'm so glad you stayed," she said to Mama, "but by now, we know what to expect, don't we?"

We stayed about a week in this school camp. There were a lot of problems. Nobody was used to this kind of living. We missed everything, especially pads for our monthly cycle. We had a few spares in our backpack but that was not enough for four girls in our family, Mama included. There had been quite a few in the suitcase that was stolen at our house, it was too bad. We asked around but nobody had spares. Then, in the gym room we found a pile of colored numbers made of cotton, which had been strapped on the chest when games were played. By folding them over and over they proved to be a big help. They came in colors of red and blue and on Royal holidays we would hang the Dutch flag in red, white, and blue on the washline, which caught a lot of smiles.

It was very hot and uncomfortable in the school, especially sleeping on the hard floors. But after a couple of days the men and boys in the camp carried in mattresses so that this problem was solved. They said they had picked them up in the streets but we thought nothing of it. This improved matters a lot, but we still had no *klambus* so the fight with the mosquitoes continued.

Occasionally some Japanese officers came in and talked with the same ladies from the main office. People started to make plans for the future. Apparently the occupying forces had the same idea. We could not stay here. Laundry facilities were not available. In the tropics, where clothes are changed at least once a day, this proved to be a disaster. There were no tubs, no washlines, no soap and in most cases not even clothes to be washed beyond the ones on our bodies. The place smelled awful. Arrangements had to be made to go somewhere else. Some people received permission to live together in a large villa, but they had to be registered by the Japanese. All the government people had to move to the governor's house, which was enormous and could hold quite a few families. Petra and her mom went there also, as her father worked for the government. I never saw her again.

As all the villas had been plundered and wrecked, nobody had a home any more. With all the unrest in town, many mothers felt safer living together in groups. They still had that choice. Quite a few families from our church planned to live for a while in our Christian high school (H.B.S.). Approximately two hundred people joined up, plus quite a few others who had no place to go. This was supposed to be a protected camp, registered by "Nippon." A sign written in Japanese had to be put up in front of the camp.

When the day of our move came we had to walk with our luggage through the so familiar streets and we were horrified by the mess we observed. In the public school the story was confirmed that the Japanese had sent the natives into the blandas' homes to protect themselves. And that, when the plundering got out of hand, they had hunted the *rampokkers* out of the area. The result was that everything the thieves had carried had been dropped in the streets in order to get away.

We could not believe our eyes . . . : beds, mattresses, baby cribs, clothing, pots, pans, tubs, pails, good and broken dishes, furniture, curtains, materials, everything that had been ours and our neighbors' was lying in the streets. There were no natives around at all and we needed everything!

On arrival in this new "camp" we headed for the classroom closest to the washrooms! We had learned already that this was a vital decision. With our large family we needed water constantly. Space was still available and we moved in. Then the organization of this camp started!

Eight

My H.B.S. and Camp Dibbits, Camps 2 and 3

I NEVER DREAMT of living in my high school day and night. I am talking about my H.B.S., Higher citizen school. It was an ideal place for group living except for the fact that we did not have anything to live on or with. But the layout of the school turned out very well.

The large building was set back from the street by a circular driveway with gates at each entrance. Again, it was built in a large square, but the whole frontage was a solid building with very small windows and in the center were sturdy front entrance doors, which could be reached by a stately set of steps.

The classrooms were roomy with wide low windows towards the inside of the square and of course long open galleries ran alongside the rooms. On the left side they ended in the open kitchens and on the right side in a row of *mandi*-rooms and toilets of a good size. At the back of the square was a huge auditorium with a stage where we used to hold our school festivities. This large room was also very often used for meetings, conferences, and so forth in normal times.

Behind the kitchens were large storage rooms and quarters for servants which, as far as I remember, were never used, neither by us in the camp nor before the war during school times.

In the front, the school looked more like a business building and maybe that is why we were not often bothered by the Japs. Still, we realized that our restricted way of living was caused by the aggressor and in this camp we had to learn to live with strangers.

After we had picked out our room we looked at each other. We could not really settle because we had nothing to settle with! On the same day we arrived, a meeting was held by all the adults and the main topic was, what to do with all this loot in the streets. We all needed it! A very important fact was stated and well—that there was not a native in the neighborhood and nobody had seen one single enemy soldier while walking over from the public school.

Now, everybody did the same thing the next day, but I'll tell about our family. Mama went out with Ids, my brother, and one of our ministers, the Reverend Zuidema, and a couple of other strong boys, to pick up the necessary household items in the streets. In the first place they came back with more mattresses. We had taken the ones from the public school with us. We girls were advised not to venture out of the camp. Most mothers who had heard about Petra's story did not even want their daughters to join the search party. Ids said later that it had been fun! They found everything we needed and there was so much out there. It did not belong to anybody any more.

Mama and Ids made several trips and brought back pots and pans, dishes and cutlery, pails and tubs for our laundry, sheets, pillows, fabrics and much more. They even brought one of our own storage trunks back, which we had used for overseas travel. We used this trunk for the longest time as a table. There were no beds so we kept on sleeping on the floor although now that we had mattresses we were not as uncomfortable. Most furniture had been broken so we did not have a chair to sit on. When Mama and Ids arrived with a load, we girls stood at the main doors and dragged it all to our room and put it in place. When they finally came "home," our small quarters looked pretty cozy already.

The next couple of days they went out again to pick up some additional things so that in the end we could get around very comfortably except that it was all in one room. But on the other side of our room lived a family that quarreled a lot. The father was Dutch and he was there too! I don't know why he was not picked up. The mother was dark-skinned. Their three children ranged in color from very dark through medium to light. The father favored the light child and the mother the dark one and sometimes they had big arguments going on between themselves and the children, which really astonished us. After a couple of weeks some people left camp to go and live in a large villa with friends or family. The room next to us became empty and this troubled family moved in there, which gave us more privacy. Besides, I did not like that man staring at us girls at all times!

Soon we noticed that things started running in a more organized fashion. The kitchens were opened from day one and shifts were organized for vegetable cleaning, cooking, washing, and cleaning up. Meals were definitely delicious at times. One main meal was provided by the camp and breakfast and supper was for us to prepare.

Before the invasion Mama and Papa had taken money out of the bank, in cash. This proved to be a fortunate move as at this time the Dutch money value was still intact. The natives had calmed down and tried to sell their wares again. The Dutch had always been their largest clientele. Soon a baker and a milkman appeared at the school doors.

Meetings were held with all heads of households and the baker and milkman were allowed to deliver their wares but only once a day in the front hall of the camp. They also decided that everyone who could afford it would contribute a certain amount per person for the main meal. Everybody agreed. And as there were also a lot of people who did not have a cent, they were provided for of course. Quite a few Indo people lived with us for a while and they were a real help. They could go to the *passar* to buy our food and they had the nicest native recipes to make the meals attractive.

The days started to turn into the same tropical routines we had been used to and we all needed this time after the many emotions everyone had experienced in the preceding weeks. We did not hear anything about the developments of the war. We only hoped that it would not last long and we were very confident of a speedy outcome. In the meantime we kept ourselves clean, kept our kitchen shifts, and enjoyed the constant company of all our friends.

We girls also had kitchen chores to do. One day we were planning to make meatballs and we were grinding meat through a meat grinder. One of the other girls was turning the handle and I was stuffing the pieces of raw meat down. While we were talking and laughing my middle finger caught in the grinder and only when I screamed the girl stopped.

My nail was crushed and even after cleaning it very well, the next day already my finger was terribly swollen and infected so that puss came out. Another day went by and Mama said, "That nail has to come off." But where was a doctor?

We inquired and found out that Doctor Engel, a lady doctor, had gone back to her house in the Villa Park and had started up her practice again. Emmy and I walked over to her place through a completely deserted neighborhood, we did not see a soul. Apparently the natives were banned from the Villa Park.

The doctor was glad to see us but when she took one look at my finger she said, "This nail has to come off. I'll do it fast but I have no ether or antiseptics." So without further ado, she slid off my nail. I thought I was going to faint as all nerve endings are in the fingertips, but I held on. She gave some instructions for after-care and Emmy and I walked back. Mama said when we returned, "Oh, that must have been worse than having a baby!" What did I know about that? It gave me a few days of rest with my hand bandaged up, but luckily my finger healed well. What I remember most is: the empty streets and empty houses with broken windows and open crushed-in front doors with all the junk and dirt in the gardens. It was like a ghost town. What destruction!

Later we heard that Dr. Engel was picked up and put in Camp Ziekenzorg in Solo, where she could still practice. But one day, when she failed to be back in time for an unexpected visit from a Japanese general, she was beaten to a pulp by the general's aide, at the general's orders, and put in an old shed at the camp gates without food or drink for several days. Camp mates had tried to smuggle something in to her, but when she came out she had to be hospitalized for a long time. Weakened as she was after the incident, she contracted hepatitis and died from it.

Of course there was a large group of young people in our camp, mostly friends from high school. Behind the kitchens were the servant quarters, which were all locked up, but behind them was a large extension of the school grounds. Even when I attended this school before all this started, I had never been in that section. We made it our hangout. Some huge old trees, good for climbing, formed perfect seating places for reading or chatting. It overlooked the high surrounding walls of the complete premises. We could see the trains go by and dreamed about times in the future when the Japanese would be gone. We spent a lot of time in that area after the main meals, during the siesta periods, and bonded with our friends.

At times we hated our existence. Liesje came down with a case of lice and it was a real fight to get rid of them. Liesje had decided to grow her hair long until "Papa comes back." I always braided her hair and discovered them. She did not want her hair cut! The other family who still lived in our room did not clean their belongings as often as necessary. Mama had seen the little girl scratch her thick hair quite often. Living on the floor was an invitation for lice to spread. Mama had a talk with the mother of the little girl. There were no chemicals available. Together they poured some coal oil on the girls' heads. The poor things had to sit there for a couple of hours with old cloths around their heads. Then their hair was washed and washed and at least for Liesje, the battle was won! We aired all our household possessions and mattresses in the hot glaring sun for a whole day, which seemed to do the trick. We were free of them!

Sometimes families left us to go and venture out in the

outside world. They were mostly the Indo families. We could not do that; with such a large family we would need a whole house. As I mentioned earlier, we still had a choice at that time to be on our own. Although we lived in a camp, we were not officially imprisoned. But because we had so many girls, it had been safer to stay in the camp thus far.

But there came a day that we got a message to clear out because the school was needed for educational purposes again, or so we were told. We had been in this camp for almost five and a half months since the Japanese occupation. It had become quite a close community. I was sad to say good-bye to some very good friends.

We found a large villa which had been used as a pension or motel-type home. We called this place Camp Dibbits as it had belonged to that family. We moved in there with four other families. Each family had two rooms. We soon realized that living in such close quarters would require patience and tact and we also learned to hold our tongues at times of squabbles.

Bertha Harwig had her baby in July and it was a beautiful baby girl, called Jopie. She had also moved into this pension with us. We often took care of the little children when the mothers took turns shopping for provisions at the *passar* nearby. We still had our main meal together and we lived a lot on fruits and vegetables and rice. The costs were shared again.

We had already learned how to make ourselves comfortable and at times it even felt cozy, everyone so close together. We young girls could not go out very much so we made the best of our quarters. Of course the household chores had to be done and we learned fast. But in our free time we secretly watched the Japanese troops go to the swimming pool where we used to swim. It was right next to our present home, though there was quite a long stretch of open field between the properties. We could see them but they had no idea they were being spied upon. The soldiers would act like little kids when they came out of the pool and would scream and yell and hit each other with their wet bathing trunks. Then the army trucks would take off again.

We also saw buses drive by full of the Japs' prostitutes going to the hospital close by for their weekly checkups. I don't know if they were forced into this trade or if they did this voluntarily. We never found out. They looked well-dressed from a distance, but we never discovered their nationalities. At night we exercised in the large open back verandah by jumping over chairs or doing other crazy stunts. We had to make the best of our situation and we ached for something to happen.

Sometimes we could attend a church service in our former church building. At one of these services little baby Jopie was baptized, but I did not go to any services. I always made excuses because I was so afraid of the Japanese that I did not want to show my face on the streets. Just thinking of Petra gave me the chills!

Only once did we have a real scare in this camp, when one evening there was a heavy knock on our front door. This door was always locked. All the mothers went together to open it after they had told us all to hide and not come out. It turned out to be a minister, who like all clergymen, was still free. He stayed for a while to talk, but we did not come out.

When we had been in Camp Dibbits about a month, one family decided to leave us and they went to live up in the mountain resort of Tawangmangu where they owned a cottage. Apparently that house had not been *rampokked* and was in good shape so they had a place of their own. Mrs. Berger with four children thought that it was safe enough as nothing serious had happened to us yet. I said good-bye to Els, my girlfriend. I was really sorry to see her go as we never knew what was going to happen. But I would see her back in our next camp.

Our small camp Dibbits was registered by "Nippon." A sign had been up at the street all along confirming that all the Dutch citizens in the building were registered by the Japanese administration. And on Christmas morning, 1942, there was a knock on the door; a notice was delivered by a couple of policemen, to be ready within two hours to be moved to a "protected camp" by Nippon. But where? We were of course very alarmed. We had been planning a simple Christmas celebration and now this.

We were allowed to bring one mattress per person, one suitcase, and several things we needed for living. All our backpacks went, of course, stuffed full with whatever was important to us. We rolled all our clothes up tightly and packed them close together in the suitcases. We brought two tubs and pails packed inside each other filled up with mats and sheets and bound them together with washline ropes. And we brought our big trunk which held a lot of our kitchen needs. Any furniture we had acquired had to stay behind. That was fast thinking and hard work. Everything we packed had to be marked with our name and that took time also. But we did it!

The other families in our house were in the same precarious situation and several came to ask Mama what would be best to take or to leave. I went to burn my diary which I had kept to date, because I did not want it to fall into strangers' hands.

Time was up before we were good and ready. The trucks

pulled up when we were scratching the last names on some luggage. We loaded the trucks ourselves and everything went on. We helped Bertha with her luggage and also with the little children when we ourselves had to climb into the trucks. The two native policemen did not stick out one hand to assist us. They did not say much either but as soon as we were all up on the trucks, they started them and left. "Where to?" we were asking each other. What was going to happen to us now and why did we have to move on Christmas day?

Nine

To Sumowono via Klecoh,
Camps 4 and 5

HERE WE ARE on a truck, racing through our so familiar city. Mama said, "I think we are going to Purwosari," and sure enough we are speeding down this very long street in the south of Solo. Mama looks worried. Actually, it is an insult to put a lady on an old army truck. The little children seem to enjoy it. It's somewhat different of course from our regular days. Mama does not complain but this treatment does not agree with her. She has lost a lot of weight these last nine months, more than fifty pounds and it shows. I am worried about her but she is always optimistic and keeps on telling us that it cannot last long! But now we don't even know where we are going and it is Christmas!

At the end of the trip we have arrived at Klecoh, a section of town which holds a couple of hospitals, called Ziekenzorg. These hospitals are converted into camps and are full of women and children from east Java, but we don't know that yet.

We are dropped off at a certain collection point. It looks like a *tangsih* (military compound). Here we stand, with everything we own in this world, looking over the unbelievable multitude of crowds milling around. What now? Nobody tells us anything and we don't recognize a single person, there are just too many.

We sit down on our luggage and wait in the hot burning sun. After a little while we start noticing what they are doing. Apparently we have to be registered. Not far from where we sit people are standing in line. Mama finds out that there are a couple of Japanese who, assisted by some native clerks, write down names and hand out numbers. So, we stand in line, dragging our possessions with us.

When we receive our individual numbers we are told to wear them day and night or else! What? We don't understand. Then we find a room to stay, in the again squared-off buildings.

I remember that this Klecoh camp was terribly crowded and dirty; that trucks and buses were constantly leaving with women and children on them and also that trucks were coming in continuously with new families on them, who had just been picked up.

We stayed here two days. People in our room told us that we were going to the mountains but where, nobody knew. I am sure we had taken some provisions with us, but the Japanese sent food in also.

Very early in the morning—it was still pitch dark—we were loudly awakened by a loudspeaker and told to take our mattresses out and throw them on the waiting trucks. It was the Sunday after Christmas. We had some breakfast and then we waited and waited for our number to be called. Buses drove off and on and women and children were loaded in. From 5:00 in the morning till mid-afternoon we waited all packed up, which was very hard for the little children as they had to stay near us at all times. Ids had gone ahead with most of the bigger boys on the luggage trucks to, they said, "unload the luggage at the other end." He was only eleven years old. Mama was really worried about him.

The time came when our number was called, no names, just a number! We made sure that all our belongings were loaded on the trucks and then we ourselves boarded a bus. The buses were loaded chock-full and off we went. Where to? This was the question on everybody's lips. Why did we have to go anyway? What were the Japanese going to do with all these women and children?

It was a terribly long and bumpy ride. All the people were desperately anxious and afraid. The screaming Japs, the panicky moments of being rushed and pushed, the unusual transport in these crummy buses and this all in the humid heat of the rainy season, it caused a lot of women to be worn out. If only we knew what was ahead of us! But they told us nothing. Several times our bus overheated and we had to stop. At one point on the way it broke down completely. We had to get out with all our hand luggage and wait on the road to transfer to another bus that eventually picked us up.

Finally we entered a mountainous area. Some people mentioned a name: Sumowono. We had never heard of it. It was supposed to be somewhere on a mountain range in central Java. When we stopped we had arrived at a rather new police training center. Nice fresh air. We noticed Ids right away among the women and children already there welcoming us at the gates. All the people on the arriving buses filled the place right up. The air was cool, the barracks looked rather new and over all it was pretty clean. Quite a few of our friends from church and school ended up here also. This was our fifth camp, but now we were under the Japs' personal "protection."

This camp was big. It was built on the slopes of a mountain range, terrace wise. There were long covered galleries running from barrack to barrack with steps in between as the whole camp sloped down hill. Alongside the galleries ran a paved roadway. They said this mountain range was above Ambarawa in central Java. There were six barracks to the left and six to the right of the camp, with some patches of grass in between where we could dry our clothes. In the center part of the camp were some rows of storage rooms, then down hill the kitchens, below them the horse stables (empty). There was a barbed wire fence around the whole complex. At the back and sides the barbed wire was not covered with *gedek* (woven bamboo slats). We had a beautiful view all around over the whole valley between the mountain ridges. It gave us a false sense of freedom, although the view was well appreciated.

Each barrack held about sixty-five people, more or less, depending on the size of the families, which made an appoximate total of eight hundred women and children. There were bunk beds on each side of the room along the walls and a middle aisle ran through the length of it. A front and back door and four side doors formed the entrances.

Everything looked pretty new. The floors were solid concrete. The washrooms were down the hill in two long rows. A little stream took the dirt away, not bad and we had lots of running tap water. Each barrack had one tap in the front. The reason why I describe this camp so extensively is because we lived here the longest time of our internment, a year and three months. We had rather good times here in the beginning but steadily it became worse and worse.

We had four bunk beds in the center part of the second barrack to the left, near a side door. Outside that door we kept our laundry tubs and pails and a little *anglo* (earthenware barbecue used with charcoal) to heat water for tea or coffee. We also had a window in our stretch of the barrack, which made it somewhat lighter inside. The roof was galvanized steel, which was terribly noisy when the tropical rains came down. Sometimes the water would run down the walls and formed big puddles on the floors. We arrived in the middle of the rainy season and up in the mountains it could be fiercely cold, especially at night. We had no blankets but had managed to bring some flannelette and cotton sheets which we doubled up for warmth. We did not have enough *klambus* either, but that was just a risk we had to take. There was also electric light but only a few light bulbs per barrack and they had to be shaded in case of air attacks!

When we settled in, we placed two bunk beds lengthwise along the middle aisle, one at the beginning of our assigned space and one at the end. Now we had a center squared-off spot before the window for living. We placed our big trunk there as a table and storage bin. In the beginning we were still allowed to hang curtains or sheets or *tikers* (woven bamboo curtains or mats) around our living area. That made it all much cozier and sort of private, although it did not diminish the sounds and noises of some seventy people in the same room. That was something we really had to get used to! The constant mumble of people talking, the crying of children, the singing, the whistling, the yelling, the clattering of dishes, the traffic through the middle aisle —mention it, it was there. It was hard to rest if you had a headache or felt sick!

My girlfriend Els Berger and her family were living

across from us. They had been picked up from their cottage in Tawangmangu and I was glad they were in our camp. It was so nice to see each other again.

Each barrack made up a set of unwritten rules and everyone understood that it was important to keep them. We had to live together. The most essential points were to hold the noise down to a minimum, and to keep the barrack as clean as possible. Further, everyone was requested to equally share the one and only tap in the front of the barrack, which required a lot of patience. The Japanese commander wanted a room leader for every barrack. We received instructions and orders from our camp leaders who in turn received them from the commander.

Soon we were all taken up in the organization of the camp activities. Even Mama took her turn in the kitchens cooking breakfast tapioca porridge, which looked and tasted like starch or glue. She had to get up at 4:30 in the morning to grate the raw coconut meat. The grated pulp had to be soaked in boiling water to make the coconut milk which was poured in with the boiling porridge. The porridge had to be stirred constantly with long paddle-like poles or else it would burn to the bottom of the drum. The smoke of the often wet wood made it frequently impossible to stay near the hot fires.

The huge kettles had to be lifted off the wood fires with bamboo poles stuck through two rings on the top of the kettles. That was very heavy and also dangerous when these kettles contained the hot boiling porridge. Mama's Friday morning porridge group cooked the most palatable breakfast glue. In the first months we still received a supply of *gulah-jawa,* which comes as a dark brown block of sugar made from sugar cane. At that time the porridge did not taste too bad but we sure had to get used to eating this gucky substance. The doctors said it was just filling, it had no food value at all. Eventually, we did not get coconuts in any more and then it became just pure glue! That was breakfast. When Mama came in from her shift her eyes were usually swollen, runny and very red. She also smelled badly of smoke. The *mandi*-rooms did wonders for that.

I talk a lot about meals as it became such an important lifeline or deathline for so many prisoners. At first, in this camp, for our main meal, we started out with enough rice and also some meats and vegetables for broths or *sayurs* (spiced vegetable stews). Trucks usually arrived early in the morning with produce and meats. Boys and girls had to carry the baskets from the gates to the kitchens. For a few months they came quite regularly. Sometimes a truck would drive heavy bags of sugar, rice, and flour to the storerooms but not for long. Soon the ladies and children had to do it themselves by way of improvised carts or just by carrying it. Depending on the cooks who had to get used to the large quantities to be prepared, most meals were definitely very enjoyable. And at night we often had soup for supper with whatever leftovers from the midday meal.

Once or twice a week in the early months of 1943 the *toko* (shop) was open at the head of the camp. Families who still had money could purchase some eggs, extra fruit or charcoal, and so forth. Only once in a while we bought some charcoal to be able to use our *anglo* and also mostly fruit. We could not buy much more because we needed so much for our large family. Mama did not know how long our money had to last. A few times Red Cross parcels arrived, but there was never enough for the whole camp. The medical supplies in it went to the little clinic. We strongly suspected the Japs of keeping the parcels for their own use! Everything was divided per person, so sometimes we received a couple of small cans of liverpaste or cheese, which we kept as a special treat for birthdays. Still, for eight people it was a tantalizing iddy-biddy. In the first months we also received dry rations like rice, sugar, flour, coffee, and canned milk. We used this as extras when meals were late or insufficient. The empty milk cans we used as drinking mugs. However, these extras were provided only in the first few months and later on they happened to come in on rare occasions. By then we had already learned how to make the most of these surprises.

In the first months some fresh milk came in and our family of eight was entitled to three quarters of a liter, mainly for the little ones. With our own rations of rice we cooked on occasion a big pot of rice porridge made with milk. That was always a nice extra meal when the food supplied by the kitchens had been miserable. We all had chores to do as hygiene in the tropics is most important.   In the valleys and cities illness was a daily threat. I also took my turns one morning per week cooking the breakfast porridge. The high oil drums were hard to clean, particularly when the porridge was burnt to the bottoms. We practically had to crawl inside to scrape them clean or else the next batch would burn again, but it had to be done.

So the first months went by with a lot of new impressions and experiences. What bothered everyone most was that we did not hear a thing about the war, that the gates were closed, the guards stood in the guardhouse, and we could not go outside! We were prisoners!

Ten

Sumowono continued

SOLO WAS a city full of schools, from a tremendous teachers' college to the simplest native public schools. And all these schools needed teachers, lots of teachers. Most of the lady teachers were interned in our camp where practically all of the people were from Solo. These ladies held a meeting and they decided that the horse stables would be very suitable as a school building.

Luckily we were in the mountains and seldom had unexpected visits from the Japanese headquarters. So very soon after our arrival the teachers set up a complete public school system, which proved very beneficial for the younger children. Ann, Ids, and Liesje went also. It kept them occupied during the day and it gave the mothers a break. There also were quite a few high school teachers but the older children had their regular camp chores as fire-wood carriers, kitchen cleaners, camp sweepers, bathroom scrubbers, mother's helpers. That's why it was impossible to set up classes for them.

The horse stalls had been set up as classrooms with

boards over crates and there was lots of room. It was a little noisy but the children were used to that from living in barracks. A lot of learning was done by heart. There was only a limited supply of paper as we were all plundered in Solo and did not have much. When writing books were full they were erased in order to be used again and again. Overall, the school was a great success!

On Sundays we even had some church services in the horse stables where one of the ladies would read a message or sermon. The services were always very well attended and constant prayers went up for a speedy end to the war and to our imprisonment. Once a real minister came in to preach a sermon and to baptize a couple of babies who had been born after we were put in this place. When the minister saw how we all lived in the chock-full barracks, he had tears in his eyes and could not believe we had to live this way!

Of course, there were daily duties for each one of us. Emmy and I did the laundry and that involved carrying a lot of water. Ids helped quite a bit. We washed beside our patch as almost all mothers with small children kept their tubs and pails near and under the one and only tap of the barrack. We had to have a lot of patience when we wanted to fill a pail of water. You can imagine the tension at times when some women refused to remove theirs.

We took care of the little ones and when Mama was very tired she used to talk things over with me, as she used to do with Papa. I really felt the responsibility at those times. Even in captivity, children don't pretend and they had to be corrected or scolded at times.

I remember that once we had a real problem. Little Elly always went to sleep with her *poh-poh*, diaper, in her case a soft silky cloth. She used to turn it over and over against her

cheeks and in this way fell asleep. It was her comfort cloth.
Well, this cloth was worn out. It was matted together by
dirt. We couldn't wash it any more, it fell apart. I said, "We
have to throw it out and get her another one." Mama said,
"You can't do that, she'll scream the whole room down." I
said, "We have to." Mama said she could not handle it.
"You do it," she told me.

I found a similar silk slip. Then I took little two and a
half-year-old Elly with me outside; I gave her the new cloth
while I took the old one out of her little hands and said,
"This is Elly's new *poh-poh* now, the old one is dirty! You can
cry as hard as you want. The old one is gone but you have a
new one! When you are finished crying, you can come in!"
and then I left her there. She made the roof come down!
Minutes later it became quiet and little Elly walked into our
living space, still whimpering and teary-eyed, but holding
her new *poh-poh* to her face. Mama and I looked at each other
and smiled. So we discussed several incidents and tried to
find solutions for our large family.

For our young people's social life we joined a gym club.
Most of the teenage girls participated. We practiced under
the skillful guidance of a physical education teacher who
got a kick out of our enthusiastic group of young girls. She
was a spirited person of Swiss origin, married to a Dutch
man, and had come from Celebes. She was full of ideas for
us. We indeed enjoyed this part of camp life. It kept us fit
and made us forget our imprisonment for a while.

We were a good three months in this camp when the
order came to hand in all our money. Instead we would receive a card with which we could shop at the *toko*. "Besides,"
said the camp commander, "you all are completely taken
care of by 'Nippon,' you don't need money." They had al-

ways checked how much we spent in the *toko*, so Mama handed in the sum of money she usually spent. She hid the rest and kept it, come what may.

With the Queen's birthday in mind (Queen Wilhelmina, on the 31st of August 1943), plans were made to hold a big party or show. We had to get permission for this from the camp commander and it was granted. He probably did not realize how the Dutch can celebrate! Then we started practicing.

On a set date all mothers and single women came to the horse stables. A stage was improvised at the end of the stables and the audience sat on upside-down feeding troughs and on boards like the schoolchildren. We had put an impressive program together. A children's choir opened the program with a series of Dutch folksongs and various happy songs, followed by little girls performing Dutch folk dances. Next came an intriguing colored-ribbon dance which was truly enjoyed by all.

Two operettas were on the bill. First a historical one, "The Escape of Hugo the Great," and then the next point on the program was the performance of the operetta *Carmen*, with a complete "Lazy Bull Ferdinand" and "Bullfighter." A group of schoolchildren and older teens were involved in this show. The music was made by mouth harmonicas and the children hummed the tunes on paper-covered hair combs, which had a fabulous effect. The costumes were made by hand from scrap paper and materials. It sounded so realistic and everyone gave it his best. The audience applauded as they never had before and between scenes they spontaneously sang our Dutch folksongs again.

The finale was performed by eight young girls (myself and Emmy included). The other girls were all high school friends and also belonged to our gym club. We danced the ballet performance of our life. The music was played on a small gramophone. Whoever had thought of bringing such an item into the camp must have had a great love for music, not realizing what camp life was all about. But it worked! We had sewn our own tutus from white mosquito-netting material stiffened with sugar and a white spaghetti-strapped top completed the costume.

I've never heard a more wholehearted applause from our mothers and friends after we finished our dance. We felt so proud. The whole evening was a complete success. I noticed some native soldiers (*heihos*) of the guards watching in the back and they were also laughing at some funny parts of the show.

But . . . very soon after this evening the order came from "higher-up," "No more shows, no more school, no more gym, no more church, no more meetings unless with the guards, no more nothing!" Instead, we had to work harder, forever be busy, no leisure time at all and we would get more surveillance on top of that, more checks by the camp commander. We had been lazy, which was an insult to the Emperor! said the Jap.

It was a great disappointment but the memory of our beautiful evening had given us a tremendous boost. Everyone secretly started doing projects on a smaller scale. There were secret craft groups, bridge groups, and we older girls started reading English books. We came together more often in our barracks just to be sociable.

We always tried to lift our spirits by doing something different; for example, we went very easy on our provisions and saved them for special occasions such as birthdays.

Even before our big party we were making special treats

on our own *anglo*. Mama had an easy cake recipe which we tried out in a six-inch aluminum cooking pot. On a low charcoal fire in the *anglo* and with some hot coals on top of the lid, our cakes were a cinch! With a little sugar and strong coffee we fabricated the icing. Very strong coffee extract was beaten with a spoon full of sugar which produced a delicious "coffee-clap," a nice foamy icing (try it!). On Mama's birthday at the end of March we served our first cake and soon many more delicious smells filled the barracks. Mama and Papa always held big birthday parties in "the good times." Now several friends came to wish Mama a happy birthday. They could not believe there was birthday cake! Everyone wanted the recipe and the method and it worked! We kept up these special treats until it was forbidden to cook privately. We always tried to remember birthdays by doing something special. Little handmade gifts were produced. For example, I made several triple bags out of the good parts of old sheets. I embroidered them with typical camp scenes. They could be hung at the side of our bunks to hold small items and were very handy.

Of course, now that the school was closed, all the children were around the barracks during the day and it was very much busier and noisier again. I was asked by the wife of one of our ministers to help out with her six children. I went every day for a while. She was the wife of the reverend who had helped Mama get back some household items in the streets of Solo. She really could not cope and everything was too much for her. So I changed wet beds, did dishes, helped with the laundry and generally cleaned up, and also watched the children. She was so grateful! She wanted to pay me but she also had no money anymore. She often gave me yarn or a piece of fabric or a sheet so that we could hand-sew shorts for all our girls. I also did the laundry, all

Eight Prison Camps

by hand, for another young woman with two babies, who had no idea how to keep house. That was a terribly dirty job!

While in this camp I turned eighteen, an age which had always seemed magical to me. Now I could only dream about what could have been, about boyfriends, school, and about what my future would hold when the Japanese would be gone. I sometimes realized so intensely that we were imprisoned, how my young teenage years vanished, that I was sad and depressed. Mama said that this mood came from our irregular lifestyle but I felt that this time was lost.

And it did not get any better. We had more visits by Japanese officers, sometimes just at the entrance gates and guardhouse, sometimes they came through the barracks. More and more orders and commands were circulated after such visits. At one time an order came for all the girls over sixteen to wear red armbands with some Japanese emblems on them. It made Mama very anxious and nervous. "You never know what they have in mind," she said. "Just stay away from the front gates, and don't show yourself!" Besides all the daily disturbing orders, less and less food was brought in, which caused the meals to become thinned out. The kitchen staff tried their best but it is hard to make something out of nothing for so many people.

After August the *toko* was closed. We still had charcoal and secretly we made some extra flour porridge from our provisions as the meals were not sufficient any more for a growing family. We sneaked in an occasional cake to boost our spirits, but soon we ran out of flour. Then we tried tapioca flour and that worked for a while. But we ran out of charcoal and private cooking was also forbidden. It seemed that all pleasures were taken away from us.

Soap was another problem. Once in a blue moon in the

first months we had received stick soap. So many inches per person. We only used it to wash the dirty spots, but Mama knew about another method. She sent us to the kitchens with a pail to collect clean wood ashes. We poured water on it, gave it a good stir and then left it alone so that the ashes sank back down to the bottom of the pail.

When the water was clear we poured it off and soaked our dirty clothes in this water overnight. It felt really soapy as wood ashes contain soda. Our clothes did not need so much of the stick soap and we could do longer with our supply. People always asked Mama how in the world our clothes on the washline could still look so bright and clean.

When told what to do, a lot of wood ashes were picked up from the kitchens, which also helped to clean out the ovens. But some ladies did it wrong and dumped all the ashes in with the clothes, only to discover that their whole laundry had turned grey! When they found out what they had done wrong and corrected it, they would also enjoy a somewhat brighter wash. We used this method all through our camp years, as long as there were wood fires.

From the very beginning there had been quite a few women and children who could not eat the camp food because of previous health problems, or they were just not used to the type of food. Their problems multiplied when our rations were cut so drastically after August, 1943. These people already showed signs of undernourishment and we ourselves were running around with tight stomachs, every day more and more realizing that something was wrong. The younger children especailly started to be whiny and cross, always asking for food. Most mothers had nothing to give, we were stuck inside the camp.

Our little ones did not grow, we noticed, there was a

standstill in their development. Elly had turned three in August and Peter was almost five but they were of the same height, quite pale and thin. They always had colds. Some people asked if they were twins, they just did not grow. Mama was so worried and we often discussed what in the world we could do to get some more nourishing food for them and of course for us all.

We older ones felt it too. We were drained at times, had no energy, and when our chores were done, we just lay down on our bunks. Then a good friend of ours lost one of her little girls. She always had been a child with eating problems and had not been able to stomach the harsh camp food. Some women with the same problems died also. Everyone became more vulnerable to contagious illnesses such as dysentery, diarrhea, mumps and measles. And the clinic was running out of medicine.

Visits of the high Japanese officers became more and more frequent. We had to take down all our privacy mats, curtains, and sheets before they did their rounds through the barracks. Then we had to line up before our patch in the center aisle. Before the delegation entered our barrack, the room leader would yell, "*Kiwotsuke*," which means, "Attention!" We straightened up. Then a scream, "*Keirei*" (bow). We stayed bent over till all the boots and samurai swords had gone by. When they were leaving the barrack, our room leader would have to yell, "*Naore*" (at ease).

We used to make ourselves look sloppy with ruffled hair and sullen expressions on our faces, for we had heard rumors about other camps where girls had been picked up to serve in Japanese bordellos to please the "poor" needy Japanese soldiers. Luckily none of our girls were ever taken out of our camp, but later we heard dreadful stories. Three girls from one family were taken out of one camp. One of them committed suicide in a prison where she was put because she refused to cooperate. Another came back after the war with a Japanese baby and what happened to the third, I don't recall. Maybe we were just lucky to be so high up in the mountains.

At one visit of Japanese officers something happened which made us think. A girlfriend of ours stood bowed over beside her mom in their barrack that day, when one of the passing officers suddenly said loudly, "Hello Miepie!" She felt a shock go through her body and when she dared look up, she recognized this officer as her hairdresser from Solo. There had been quite a few Japanese barbershops and beauty salons in town before the war, as well as department stores and other shops.

Miepie was born with a wild, bushy, blond, curly head of hair, which forever had to be trimmed as it grew so fast. Every week for years she had visited this hairdresser. She discovered in this way that this man must have been a Jap spy before the war started. Why else would he now show up as a high ranking officer for the women's camps? Could he have accomplished the rise in status from hairdresser to this position in a year's time? We doubted it! When she told us about it we could not believe it.

I remembered at that time that Papa also had his hair cut at this shop and that, not long before the war, he had come home with a strange story: While he was in the chair for his haircut, a modernly dressed Japanese lady had walked into the shop. All the barbers had been quite excited and had talked vividly and loudly in Japanese to her. She had sat down in a barber chair behind a screen and . . . one of the barbers had started to shave her! Papa said, "I could not believe my eyes but they did shave her." Now, when I remembered this story I wondered with my friends, "Would she have been a he? Also doing undercover work, like spying?" Gradually it became clear to us that we had been outwitted and too trusting. Our suspicions proved to be true after the war. We heard that a lot of Japanese businessmen had been involved with spying while living in the Indies.

One day we received an order to hand in our valuables, which most of the Solo people did not have anyway. We had to hand in cameras and movie cameras, flashlights, radios, and anything with wires or batteries in it. Further, important papers, photo albums, diaries, any kind of writing paper, passports, ownership papers, mortgages, insurance papers, books, whatever! Most people handed them in.

One of our high school teachers who lived at the end of our barrack came around to tell us that she felt as if she just had committed a murder! When we asked, "Why?" she said, "I have just destroyed my movie and my two other cameras. If I cannot have them, he [the Jap] is not going to have them either!" She almost cried for they were expensive articles with a lot of memories.

Mama sewed all our valuables in the crotch of a panty. I knew there was some money in it and some gold watches and rings, but also all our birth certificates. She had done it just in time, for if all these anxieties were not enough, we got a room search out of it. We were chased outside in the sun while our possessions were poked and prodded and squeezed. They took our one and only emergency flashlight which had been so handy going to the toilets late on dark rainy nights.

Soon after that, the order came to hand in, supposedly for "safe keeping," all gold, silver and jewelry. We had only the rings on our fingers and some watches. I hid my rings in the lining of my backpack and they were never found!

All these measures upset us greatly in our already un-dernourished condition. This happened at the end of 1943. We knew nothing about the developments of the war, but it sure made us think that something was amiss. What would the enemy do with our money? They had brought in their own Japanese currency already. Not that we had used it but one way or other we had heard about it from new-comers. A few times we had air-raid alarms and were com-pletely blacked out. Many nights we sat in completely pitch-dark barracks.

Something must have been going on as the visiting Japs became meaner and meaner and screamed louder than ever, "You should be more grateful for all the good things Nippon provides for all the lazy ladies," was a regular repertoire. We never knew what would be next on the agenda. Usually it was punishment, with less food to be brought into the camp and we were eating only thin rice soup by then. Or no wood would come in at all, so we could not cook!

What happened at Christmas and New Year, I don't re-member. I suppose not much, as everything was forbidden and our energy was gone. After a year and three months (ac-tually it was on Ids' birthday, the 23rd of March, 1944), a bunch of rough Japs entered our camp. And yes, we were chased out of our barracks as we were getting another search. All morning we stood in the burning sun. We could not take anything out of our room with us, but one of us was wearing the "pants!" Before they started, for some rea-son or other, one of the barrack leaders was beaten up by one of the Japanese soldiers. We were scared, as the "searchers" were in a foul mood. They made an awful mess in our barrack which we had to clean up. Besides, when they left we received the message, "Yes, be ready early tomorrow morning, you are moving to Ambarawa." What a shock! We had hoped to stay in this camp till the war would be over, but no, it was not in the cards. We scurried to pack our poor possessions and worked till midnight. We packed up everything we owned. We said, "We'll throw it all on the trucks, they can only refuse it," and to our surprise, the coolies (native laborers) loaded it all on. The soldiers stood behind them with a whip, shouting their best word in Malay, "*Lekas, lekas, lekas!*" All Bertha's luggage went too, we helped her with it. The question was, would we see it again? We went in buses. Where would we go in Ambarawa? It was not too long a ride but our hearts beat anxiously. What would this move bring?

Eleven

Ambarawa 2, Camp 6

I DON'T REMEMBER how long the bus ride was from Sumowono to the next camp in Ambarawa. I know we stayed in
mountainous regions all the time but I don't even remember
at what time we arrived. I only remember the entrance gate.
It was a high old wooden one.

A lot of the Sumowono people went to other camps.
We were unloaded outside this camp and had to walk inside
through the gate. After being counted, we were taken to a
barrack by a woman along long stretched *empers*. It seemed
that our appointed room was full already. All the women
and children had to move in closer together so that our family of eight could be added. That made sixty-nine in that
room.

The next day we had a search and in the same week a
second. We did not even have a chance to settle in, but they
did not find anything on us. It was so disturbing! What were
they after? And then by the end of that week the whole
camp had to assemble on the sports field. After all the rig-
marole of standing to attention and bowing deeply, we were

told that from now on we were officially under military rule and would be called prisoners-of-war. Yippee!

We got a new camp commander out of it, a tall Korean Jap with wiry glasses, who always used to beat up the ladies for the least little error or simple mistake. The Japanese from Korea were generally taller and much more sadistic. Only the Japs who belonged to the *kempei tei* (military police) could outdo the Korean Japs in their malicious treatment of prisoners. This man promptly got the nickname: Brille-Jap (Spectacles-Jap).

From then on we gradually discovered what this camp was all about. I think that it had been an old hospital, and old and dirty it was! We met lots of other women and children again, all new faces. Most of our former camp mates ended up in the other barracks. This camp was built completely different than Sumowono. There were lots of barracks built criss-cross over the compound all connected by *empers*. The barracks were brick buildings with tiled floors, but the buildings were old. Ours ran parallel to the outside barbed wire fence in the back of the camp, which was covered with eight-foot high *gedek*, so we could not see the outside world. There were strips of dead grass between the barracks and along the barbed wire fences people had developed a few little gardens with mostly tomato plants.

As newcomers we were assigned the worst spots inside the room, but that was something we did not complain about. It is to be expected when you come into a new camp. We had four places right in the center, at the entrance of the only side door and three across from the side door, so the traffic was continuous. Ids had to go to a barrack for boys only, supervised by two tough women.

One door at the end of the barrack was permanently

closed and at the other end the door led to the next room. We had one-and-a-half bunk beds, to sleep four of us. And one large all steel double (so called Singapore) bed, which even came with a *klambu*. Three of us slept there. Space between the beds was minimal and space to sleep was equally minimal!

The trucks with our mattresses and other luggage arrived intact and everything was there. Of course we were right up front to find our possessions and took them all to our room. The people were nice enough and wanted to know everything about our former camp. We told them that we had been sorry to leave but that the supply of food had been terrible. They informed us that we should not expect anything better here in this camp, especially with approximately four-hundred extra people.

Our neighbors beside the bunk beds were two spinsters who were vegetarians and they were really suffering as none of the foods they were used to were available. Beside them was a family of five. The oldest boy was around sixteen. He used to sneak out of the camp underneath the barbed wire at night and exchange some old clothes of his family with the natives for bananas, other fruits, and rice. Mama once jokingly asked his mom if he could bring something for our big family but she said it was too risky and she was right of course! If he was caught he would get a severe beating. Not very many people knew about his nightly prowling.

Across the aisle beside the steel bed we had a neighbor on one side, a Mrs. Laarman, the "fat lady," with two children. She was addicted to smoking and she would do anything for a cigarette. She even traded her meals for it. She never took food away from her children though. When we met her she was rapidly losing weight as the meals were already very inadequate and she did not even eat them. Her son and the other sixteen-year old also slept in the special boys barrack. The Japanese guards often wanted them to be available for odd jobs. On the other side of the steel bed lived a very young mother with two little children who whined a lot. The usual noise of a room full of women and children did not bother us any more. We also noticed that Bertha and her two children had not come to this camp and there were more friends missing who must have gone elsewhere.

A couple of mornings later, several of us woke up with the biggest hives of some sort, particularly the little ones. When Mama showed them to our neighbors, they said, "Oh, bedbugs, we all have them here." From then on the hunt was on for these creatures. Unbelievable, the wooden bunks were full of them! Every day, if it did not rain, we threw our mattresses outside in the hot sun and we took turns removing as many stinky brown bugs as possible. Did they ever reek! It made me sick!

And it did not help much, because our neighbors did not clean their beds. They were either too tired or too lazy. The "fat lady's" bunks were so infested with the bugs you could just see them crawling around and the beds were only inches apart from ours! Mama once kindly asked her if they did not bother her? She said, "I don't get bitten and my little girl neither," and she drew another puff from her cigarette. She was a very nice lady though. She walked around on her bare feet all day and used to joke with us girls about being free and taking us out for cake and ice cream.

Soon we were taking our turns in the kitchens cleaning veggies and cutting up pig heads and hoofs. All the discarded parts were apparently good enough for the women's camps. The cooks made sure that everything was boiled thoroughly to avoid spoiled soup.

In this camp we still received cooked rice portions for a while, which gave us some fill. But so much disappeared from the kitchens which was destined to be in the *sayurs* to go with the rice. When cleaning veggies, women would smuggle carrots and other salad stuff to their rooms, which was not fair. Time and time again the block leaders mentioned our poor rations but the soup or *sayur* stayed thin.

Upon the constant request of our camp leader, a very feisty lady, to provide us with more meat and vegetables, the camp commander came to the kitchens to check things out for himself. When the kitchen staff was busy preparing the big drums of food, he asked what that was in the waste baskets. When the ladies explained that was garbage, he asked, "Why is it green? You better eat it!"

From then on the carrot tops, beet tops, potato peels and anything which we used to throw out because it was rotten or dirty, had to be cooked in the soup or *sayurs*. The man himself stood over the cooking kettles making sure it went in! As all the garbage went out of the front gates and was checked, it had to be done. "As long as you are throwing out so much 'good' food, you are not getting any more in," he said.

The soup looked like an unsavory mush and often tasted bitter. More people showed up with diarrhea and other stomach ailments. We did not get any more fresh produce in anyway. Luckily our family did not suffer from the real infectious diarrhea or dysenteries very often. The little ones had slight attacks after certain rough meals but nothing serious. A lot of little children could not overcome the loose stools; many became gravely ill and many did not make it. I think our good health was due, in part, to the fact that we were all brought up not to eat anything unwashed or dirty. We could not even eat a cookie which we had dropped to the floor. Mama had contracted typhoid in the earlier years in the Indies and was very cautious. There are so many infectious illnesses in the tropics. Even in our dreadful existence we tried to keep ourselves as clean as possible and hope for the best.

A very good friend of ours with three little children lost her youngest baby boy which shook us all up terribly. So it went with a lot of other young families. Many had something wrong with them and it did not heal. Many carried the burden of fear, of not being able to make it before the war was over.

Women and children developed camp sores, open wounds that just did not want to close. I had such a sore on my leg and Emmy had a bad abscess on the side of her face. There was a little building in the middle of the camp used as a clinic. For a while we had a Hungarian doctor named Dr. Oeljaki helping out, with the assistance of some nurses. They had no medicine or ointments, no bandages or disinfectants. They cleaned hundreds of boils and camp sores with boiled water only and then advised us to go and sit in the hot sun to dry up the sore. Sometimes it worked, sometimes it did not. The doctor treated Emmy and me very professionally. We were lucky we healed. One day, all of a sudden, this doctor was gone. Nobody knew what had happened to him. But the nurses carried on with the clinic.

Not being able to get enough to eat or to get anything extra is a hopeless feeling. It certainly undermined our bodies. We had no money anymore, besides, we were not allowed to go outside the camp and could not trade through the *gedek*. There was no milk at all, which worried so many mothers who had babies and small children. Mama was one of them!

Soon after we arrived in this camp, we decided to start a small tomato patch behind our barrack. After a month or so we were able to pick our own tomatoes from our own plants. We were so proud and they were delicious. Almost every family had a little patch so there was a minimum of theft. For a while we received a little unleavened loaf of bread per person per day. The "loaf" was as big as a squared-off bun and it was as hard as solid glue. You could kill somebody with it! We had no butter or margarine, but thin, thin slices with tomato on it was a treat!

Of course the Japanese camp commander discovered all the tomato gardens and he thought that this was a great idea. He ordered a group of women to develop all the open stretches of ground along the barbed wire fences into gardens. With *patjols* (a sort of broad sided pick) the women dug and cleaned the hard clay ground. In the dry season the ground usually splits, as it hardly ever rains. The soil is then hard as a rock, but they did it and planted mainly tomatoes, green beans, and some peanuts. Most of it could be used in the kitchens but it was not much for so many people. The head of the garden group was a teacher and a good friend of ours. She often asked Mama if one of the girls could fertilize the growing plants with our night potty. So, early in the morning, I used to go by the gardens to pour a little of the "fertile juice" on the sides of the tomato plants and veggies. They said it would make the tomatoes taste sweeter, do you believe it?

We learned that the people in this camp, Ambarawa 2, also had better times before we came in from Sumowono.

When we were doing the camp chores they kept on singing or humming some cheery tunes, when the Japs were not around. When we asked, they told us that they also had celebrated a camp show. The same thing had happened as in our former camp, everything had been forbidden afterwards.

It is amazing that regardless of where women's camps were kept, the same spirit existed. This was the spirit of cheering each other up, of diverting depressed minds into more optimistic views. Our lifestyles had changed so drastically, but just a reminder of how it could be gave a lift to so many of us. It bonded us together.

But then, camp life deteriorated as time went by and we started looking into each other's plates. In large camps food distribution always was a big problem. Usually each barrack would fetch the prepared food from the kitchens, after a little boy had come by shouting, "Room 7 . . . get your dinner" (or breakfast).

Armed with large tubs and pails we would take turns picking up the food. These persons also had to ladle it out to their roommates. For our family, Emmy and I or Ann and Ids would stand in line with a couple of pots. As we received eight ladles of rice and eight ladles of soup or *sayur*, it always seemed that we were getting *so much*! Continuously it happened that the last few ladles were not as full as the first ones or, that there was a bit more shaken off before it landed in our pot. And then *we* had to divide it onto our plates when we sat down to eat.

We learned to be tactful without getting into fights with so many people in a room. Thus we decided that we were all going to stand in line with our individual plates or, four of us would go with two plates each. This way we did not have to make a fuss about the distribution of the food and we would get what we were entitled to. Hunger is a tricky thing. Other large families would protest though! The same thing happened when fruit was divided. For our large family we would get four large bananas, while a single person would receive one whole one. That was very difficult to accept. Occasionally there were leftovers in the kitchens—*very* occasionally. It happened that, in turn, a room could fetch some extras which we received as a feast.

However, the Japanese military rule over the women's camps had more and more tricks up its sleeve. Our camp leader had a hard time obeying and following up all the new orders and changes. The camp commander's hands were hard and rough and quite a few women received a sample of the casually handed out slaps for no reason at all. The worst time to run into one of them was at night. So many people had stomach ailments. When one of our girlfriends, who was only fifteen, had to go to the toilets in the middle of the night and ran into a guard, she was severely beaten up because she was not wearing her registration number. We always had to be prepared.

Our room leader, Mrs. Schenk, got into trouble one day when the Spectacles-Jap did his rounds. He found the tap for our barrack slightly trickling. The lady was called and without explanation she was slapped around. I stood in the doorway and saw it all. When her son heard about it, his friends had a hard time holding him back for he was going to attack the Jap, which would have been disastrous!

Once it happened that the Spectacles-Jap approached our whole family on his rounds when we were having our soup together on the *emper* before our barrack. We saw him coming, rose to our feet and bowed deeply as we were supposed to do. He stopped at our group and started yelling and screaming at us at the top of his lungs. We had no idea what he wanted until Ids had a brainstorm! He straightened up and shouted, "*Kiwotsuke!*" We *all* straightened up. Then Ids called, "*Keirei!*" and we all bowed. Ids again raised his voice, "*Naore!*" and without any further ado we saw him walk away. That's what he had wanted, what a puppet show! And how rude. I guess we would never get used to being screamed at!

Another sample of the Spectacles-Jap's foul mood happened one early morning. A little puppy had wandered into the camp underneath the front gates. The children of the nearest barrack were delighted. They cuddled and played with the little thing. They shrieked with laughter and chased the little dog around the small courtyard.

The gate opened and in came the Korean camp commander. Right away he yelled at the kids, scooped up the puppy, returned to the entrance and crushed the little dog's head between the gates, dead! Well, the children screamed hysterically and disappeared in their rooms to tell their mothers, of course. This story flashed through the camp like a wild fire with the warning, "Stay out of his way!" It made me think again about our dogs. What would have happened to them when we were robbed? I remembered seeing our Mollie with young Sujatih when we all left in the Jap car. And now these terrible things were happening every day. When would it end?

Twelve

Ambarawa 2 continued

After June of 1944, the situation in the camp became worse and worse. The guards roamed through the camp continuously trying to find fault with trivial matters. Everyone tried to at least look busy from weeding between stones to scrubbing toilets. The dirt had to be swept away through a small stream that ran through a concrete ditch over which rows of toilets were built. Liesje was working on this camp chore. The Spectacles-Jap had ordered the smaller girls to work too. Under the supervision of a couple of women this group of nine-to-twelve-year olds had to clean and scrub the toilets every day, which was necessary, of course. But Liesje often said that she could not believe that people were such pigs, looking at the misguided "missiles" and "bombs" *on* the stepping stones over the stream and not *in* the stream. With pails of water and *sapu lidihs* (long brooms of bamboo strips) they rinsed and scrubbed. But there were so many women and children, it was a battle to keep everything clean.

We kept a couple of pairs of wooden *tekleks* (flip-flops)

especially for going to the toilets. Normally during the day, we just went barefooted. One night I came back to bed after a trip to the toilets and just when I slipped into bed, I saw a light-giving *klabang* (centipede) crawling on my shoulder. Holding back my screams, I jumped out of bed and ripped off my nightclothes but I could not find a thing! What a scare! My heart beat in my throat. This dirty camp drove me nuts. Emmy had a similar experience. There were so many little and big annoying incidents here, no wonder there were so many stressed-out people.

In the meantime, our camp leader had to cope with the Jap. He was forever pushing her to find more work for the "lazy" women. At one time, he had asked her a question. He said in broken Malay, "When I walk through the camp I often hear the women say this particular word and I want to know what it means?" She answered, "Which word do you hear?" and he said very brokenly, "Rotjap!" (Rotten Jap). While hiding her grin she had instead looked pensive and replied politely, "No, I've never heard that before, I don't know!" The block leaders told us the story and we all got a warning to hold our tongues.

Between our fights with the bedbugs and our daily chores we were pretty tired. The steady reduction of our meals for over a year now started to influence the whole camp population. People were too tired to get up unless forced by chores. Children were either impossible or sleeping too much and there was not one thing anybody could do to improve matters.

Then the Spectacles-Jap, who definitely kept track of the mood in the camp, came up with the order of morning exercises! At 6:30 in the morning he himself conducted military exercises on the old sports field on one side of the camp. Old and young had to perform the Japanese army movements of head, arms, and legs. When some ladies stayed away, the Spectacles-Jap himself would go into the barracks to hit them personally, driving them to the field while screaming at the top of his lungs.

Here stood all these tired worried mothers and children, swinging their arms and kicking up their legs while counting aloud in Japanese, "Itji, ni, san, sji, go, roku, sitji, hatji, kju, dju!" It was pathetic and degrading. In normal times exercises are OK, but now, all these people were undernourished, a lot them were sick and had no energy. The Spectacles-Jap however, was often in a good mood after the session was over and even tried to be sociable by poking some younger ladies in the ribs!

This was also the time though for the camp leaders to approach him for special requests. Promises were made but not often kept. Instead, we got more and more house searches. They always came unexpectedly. We had to stand in the hot tropical sun while a small army of Japs went through all our things and this lasted till the whole camp was searched. One of us girls had to wear "the pants" with our papers and valuables in it. Luckily nobody was ever personally searched. There were just too many women and children. I guess they were always searching for radios or communication materials. Everything had already been handed in or found, so what were they still looking for?

At one search I had the chicken pox and I had them bad! A small epidemic of the disease had swept through camp and as I never had them as a child, my immunity was apparently low enough to contract them now that I was nineteen. When an adult gets a child's illness it always is much worse. Sure enough, I was sick, had fevers and was covered with dreadful looking black scabs. The nurses in the clinic had given me some Dermatol, a greenish-yellow powder, to dry up the blisters. I looked frightfully ugly and then we were stormed by all these small fearful-looking Japanese soldiers who frantically started searching the barracks.

As I mentioned, they always came unannounced and unexpected. Our room, being at the back of the camp, had fair warning. All our nearest neighbors stuffed valuables under my sheet and mattress, I don't even know what it all was. I said, "If they find it, I get killed!" and they said, "They'll be so scared of you, don't worry . . . ." And then they all went outside to stand in the sun. The search lasted all morning.

It was true, we knew that the Japanese were terrified of contagious illnesses and I looked horrible. Well, they did not even come close to my bed and went in a wide circle around it. I, however, had a perfect view of how they searched the room. They shook every mattress and turned them over. I secretly hoped they would catch some bedbug bites! They looked inside every suitcase, quite often turning them over also, and everything was shaken and squeezed. All of them were wearing surgical masks. In other barracks they even cut mattresses open. It was a mess!

I did not feel so safe with all that loot in my bed and I was quite anxious about it. I could count myself lucky that I had this kind of sickness or else they would have made me get up and get out. When finally it was over and they had left, everyone was very thankful to me and their comment was, "I told you so, they don't come near someone who looks so ugly!" Thanks a lot, I thought.

A couple of weeks later I had healed up quite a bit but for the longest time deep scars remained on my face. It still took me quite a while to get a bit of my strength back. The only thing to be thankful for was the fact that we were in a mountainous area. Although the days could be unbearably hot, the nights were often comfortable and sometimes even cool, which helped my recovery.

Apparently there were several women's camps in Ambarawa, central Java, that we did not know about. We had no outside connections whatsoever. We did not hear anything and we did not know anything about the war. Only by the behavior of the guards could we speculate that something was going on, but they did not tell us anything.

By the end of September, 1944, a dreadful thing happened which affected almost every family in our camp. We heard later that it happened in all women's camps. The order came from the "higher-up" for all boys ten years old and up to leave us and go to a separate boys' camp. "Why?" was the very first protest question. "Why ten-, eleven-, twelve-year-olds or any boy that is still with his family?"

The reason our camp commander gave was so silly it was unbelievable. He said that the boys could start going out with the girls and could get them in trouble, which was not allowed in a camp. Our camp leader said, "Ten-year olds, eleven-year olds? Even twelve-year olds, come now!" But he got mad and told her to tell the boys to be ready to go by the next morning!

The whole camp was upset and not a little bit. One day here, the next day gone. Ids had to go also. He was just thirteen and we loved him. The evening before the boys had to leave I went to the kitchen and borrowed an *anglo* with charcoal. With a little onion, *sambal*, which is a red-hot pepper paste, tomatoes and our day rations of rice I made a pot of *nasi goreng* (fried rice). That was our last meal together for quite a while. Mama prayed for Ids and asked the Lord to guide him and protect him when he was all alone. We all cried, for we realized that we might never see him again.

It was a sad day when the boys left. One mother had two boys, a ten- and an eleven-year-old. She stayed all alone. "Take care of each other", she called after them. But she did not cry. There were not many mothers who cried, at least not in our camp. They did not want the Japanese guards, who were standing at the gates laughing, to know how deeply they were hurt. Instinctively, nobody gave them that satis-faction.

Quite a few boys lined up at the gates and after they were counted, they marched out. Just before they disap-peared Ids looked back at us and gave us his biggest smile. Some boys even called out, "Don't worry mom, we'll be back soon!" What was to become of these young boys? Our Ids looked to be quite a sturdy boy but could it be hunger edema already? Where would they go and who would take care of them? So many questions.

Back at the barracks many tears flowed. Mama held her-self strong in front of us but she was brokenhearted. She kept on saying, "The Lord will take care of him, I am sure." And it gave us all courage again. We thought of him all day long and throughout the next days and weeks. We surely missed the boys. When they were gone our workload be-came much heavier. We had to carry wood in for the fires, carry big bags of rice, corn, and flour, and do the heavier work in the kitchens. Ids had always worked in the kitchens and now we realized how hard it had been for a little boy. At least, he had enjoyed some more food every day by scrap-ing out the cooking drums.

Once in a while, one particular Japanese guard would

walk through our camp, hands on his back, smiling at the ladies who were doing the laundry at the one and only tap at the barracks. When they jumped up to bow deeply, as required, he would smile again. Or he would stroll through the kitchens, again smiling sort of gently, without bothering anybody. What did we know about him? He was just another Japanese soldier. Was he spying on us and could we be strapped with another restriction or something?

Then rumors of the whereabouts of our boys began drifting around. Also rumors that this mysterious guard had taken some notes from mothers to their boys and vice versa. This man got the name of "Hansel my slave" (*Hansje m'n knecht*, a Dutch tale of someone who runs errands and performs good deeds). We were sure now that our boys were still in Ambarawa and we also learned that Ambarawa was full of women's camps! It made us all feel somewhat better that Ids was not too far away, although we never heard from him.

Again, I don't remember anything about Christmas and New Year's 1944. We were probably too tired to do anything about it, and at any rate, everything was forbidden. We could not stand talking together with more than two persons or else we would get in trouble. Especially after November, the camp guards really clammed up and were completely unapproachable. If I think back now, that was the time that Tokyo was bombed for the first time. It appeared to us that something was drastically wrong for our oppressors. But it was not over for us yet. In early January, 1945, we were shocked with another order, "Pack up everybody, you are moving!" Again? The camp had to be emptied. I don't remember the exact date, it was just after New Year's. We could not believe it. We could take just so much with us. No trunks or large suitcases any more. Just small ones and whatever we could carry, plus a mattress per person. And again, one day here, next day gone.

As soon as we got the message we threw our mattresses in the hot sun and kept them there all day. This time we all searched and killed most of the bedbugs, hoping not to take them along to whereever we would go.

One thing was certain, these moves were always done purposely to try and break up possible conspiracies. We never saw a lot of people from this camp again. The trucks came early to collect the luggage. I have no idea how we were sorted out and I still suspect it went by registration number. We loaded our possessions onto the trucks and shoved everything on. Nobody was counting. Instead of our table-trunk, we had collected some fruit baskets from the kitchens to pack our cooking pots and mats etc. We also took a chance and packed our small laundry tub and pails together into a basket and tied them together, again with the washlines and kept our fingers crossed. We needed everything with our large family. And it all went. The trucks took it all! But where was it going?

After the trucks left, we had to assemble at the gates to be counted, which was quite an effort on the part of the Japs. We apparently went in groups because when we arrived at the gates quite a few people were walking already on the road.

We had to walk out of this camp!

Thirteen

Moving Again

I AM WALKING on a street, a real street, in Ambarawa. This is the first time since September, 1942, when we walked in the streets of Solo from the H.B.S. camp to Camp Dibbits. Now it is January, 1945, we have been two years and four months behind *kawat* (barbed wire). But we are still not free to go, even if they make us walk out of this camp.

I am loaded. I am carrying my backpack which is stuffed full with my personal belongings, toothbrush included. From it dangle several items like a small saucepan, for boiling water, some tools for emergencies, and a small blanket. We have learned to keep necessary household items with us, just in case our luggage gets lost. Mattresses and larger luggage are impossible to carry on a long stretch. It is a risk we have to take when we load it on the trucks. Thus far we've only lost a couple of mattresses and a few smaller items. I'm glad we took all the essential things with us. The Japanese camp commander is very impatient to get us out of this camp, Ambarawa 2. Only small suitcases are allowed. Our trunk/table and a large chest have had to stay behind. We tried to shake some silver coins out of the trunk which we had sunk between the lining before all the searches started, but to no avail. There was not enough time!

Besides my backpack, I am carrying a small suitcase for the little ones in one hand and in the other hand a heavy basket stuffed full with a cooking pot and some big spoons, some lengths of stick soap and a couple of sheets. The sheets are important, we can make a lot of clothes out of them. We have packed everything tightly, rolled it up so that we could take more. It is hard to pack from a large suitcase into a smaller one. We packed the baskets and nobody stopped us.

All these thoughts whirl through my mind while I am following the other women and children on the road. "Where are we going? Why do we have to walk this time? Maybe we are going to the next camp here in Ambarawa. There are supposed to be quite a few."

I am so tired. We have all worked so hard packing and getting ready. The muscles in my shoulders and neck are cramping together. I have to go on, though. I look back at the others. Mama is talking to the little ones. It is so hot. I guess it must be around noon, at least it is not raining. The children do not carry anything. They are four and six now, but they are so small and thin and pale, poor things! Ann and Liesje are with Mama. They are carrying backpacks and bags. Mama has her hands free for the little ones. Emmy and I are ahead.

I should go slower, my neck is so sore, but I *have* to bring this *barang* (luggage). We will need it as soon as we arrive, but where are we going? Mama has a couple of bottles of water. I am so thirsty, but I am not going to ask, I'll wait till we are there. Keep your feet moving! My neck is all cramped up. I don't know this town at all. We have never been outside Camp 2. I don't see anyone stopping up ahead. Where are we going?

I am still following the line of prisoners ahead of me. It feels like everyone has slowed down. It is still so hot and I am not feeling well. My load seems to get heavier and I cannot stop. How long have we been walking now? Boy, am I stiff, my neck and head refuse to cooperate. If I could only rest for a minute. I see no guards around. Mama keeps on calling, "Stay together please," and we do. Maybe I should have put more on the trucks. Nobody complains, we just move on.

A woman just passed us and mentioned, "It's not very far any more. We are going to the train station." The train! Mama tells it to the little ones and it gives them a boost. They step a bit quicker and babble about going in the train, something new! I don't know how long we have been walking, but my neck is killing me.

People are stopping in the distance. That must be the station. My goodness, there is hardly any shade up there and no train either. Are we really going by train? Everyone is sitting down in the full sun, glad to drop their heavy loads, I guess. But the guards are yelling and screaming, I can hear them in the distance. Poor mothers with small children. They had to put everything on the trucks in order to be able to hold on to their kids. So they have practically nothing with them to comfort the children.

The station is just an overhang over an open platform. Not enough for all these people to get some shade. We finally join the crowds. The Japanese and *heihohs* make us go into a squared-off area used for cattle or sheep. They make us sit down close together. I'm glad I can drop my load. My neck and shoulders need a break so badly that I am light-headed. We did not have much to eat this morning, but I would rather have some water now. Mama sits down and we all come for our drink, a few sips, we don't know how long this day will last! What would Ids think if he knew that we are leaving? Maybe it is best that he does not know. We are all silent and with the others we wait.

The sun is hot. We have a few sun hats, but there is no relief. I could drink some more but it has to be saved for the trip. Where is the train? Again, the guards come shouting around telling us to sit down and wait, which we are already doing. How long till this train comes? One hour, two hours? The children are getting restless. The sun is white-hot now. There aren't many guards around now. Mama suggests we nibble on some pieces of dry glue bread, which makes our thirst worse.

A rustle goes through the crowds. People are getting to their feet. "The train, the train. . . ." We hear a soft rumble and yes, in the distance a locomotive is in sight. Now we are all standing. Slowly a train pulls up alongside the platform and comes to a squealing stop. It is steaming hot and it looks like all the windows are boarded up with wooden slats.

The women and children are picking up their *barang*, but here come the guards, ordering us, screaming at the top of their lungs and shouting in Japanese and Malay to sit down again, to hide and cover our faces. And also to sit with our backs towards the train. Why? We do drop back and sit. The soldiers are standing threateningly over us with the bayonets on their rifles. We are sitting somewhat on the side in this area. I have my head down between my knees and my sun hat on top, but I can sneak sideways glances and have a good look of the train.

Now the doors of the train open and slowly out come old gray men in all shapes and sizes. Old they are and they barely move. They are shabbily dressed. Some of them are leaning on others, some are on stretchers and are carried out by four or more old men. What a tragic sight! They see us but there is no contact, no smiles, no recognition. They are a heap of misery.

The guards and *heihohs* rush them off to the other side of the station. At least there are trucks waiting to take them away, but not until the train is completely empty, which takes a long time. Would they be going to our camp, Ambarawa 2, where we came from? Poor, poor men.

The attention of the soldiers on us slackens off. Several are called away and more and more women take a peek at what is going on. The whole afternoon has gone by and the sun is almost gone. The last trucks with the old men are pulling away. And we sit here in this burning humid heat. Then it becomes dark...

Suddenly the Japanese officer in charge remembers that we are still here. The yelling starts all over again, *"Lekas, lekas!"* They point to the train. Everyone struggles to his feet. Like a herd of cattle they chase us towards the platform and make us board this train where all those sick old men just came out, with all their illnesses and contagious germs. I do pity the old men, but the train is not even cleaned out or aired through. But there are so many people, it does not go that fast. Our family is in the back of the line-ups. We even have a chance to walk around a bit on the platform.

While there, we notice some young boys in the distance busy unloading the freight cars of the train. They carry bags of rice, grain, and so forth, and load them on a truck by the light of a small overhead bulb. Emmy says, "I see Ids!" and then both of us see him waving under the light. We do the same, we stand under the light bulb on our side of the platform and we wave and wave! Then he is gone, but we saw him! We are happy, now he knows at least that we are leaving. Maybe it *is* better to know.

Eight Prison Camps

We tell Mama and the others while we climb into the train. Mama smiles and asks questions, but that was it, we just saw him and waved. Our first reaction after entering the smelly passenger car is trying to open the windows, but most of them don't budge, they are nailed closed. Oh, does it ever stink in here and is it hot! Some air comes in through the open doors but even if it is early evening it is not much cooler outside!

What is all this yelling and cussing about? Are the old men finally getting up to protest their cruel treatment? No, it's the guards again. What now? Nobody understands. Oh, they are entering the cars . . . .

"Shut the windows, close the windows. He wants them shut!" goes the call through the cars. Do we have to sit in the dark in this stinking train, in this hot muggy air? We follow orders. Why not? The windows are boarded up on the outside anyway, but somebody must have tried to open them. Who wants to get beaten up on a day like this? Nobody dares to touch the windows again. And there are no lights inside the train car! The boarding of the women and children with all their luggage takes some time. We are trying to find a seat in the dark.

Each car gets a guard at the door. We are ending up in the center of the car. They are fourth-class train cars, wooden seats along the sides and we are pushed in. It's crowded. We put our *barang* up on the racks as much as possible. In the dark Mama asks us to try and check if the floor is relatively clean as the children have to sit there. When we have to go to the one and only latrine at one end of the car, we have to step and struggle over all the bodies on the floor. The latrine is just a hole in the floor of the train car and the dirt simply falls on the rails. The putrid smell is sickening and the dirty shiny flies and bugs are uncountable.

Now everyone is waiting in this oven, trying as usual to make the best of it all. The hot musty air we must breathe is scary but the calmer we keep ourselves the less it will affect us. It seems that everyone else is trying to do the same. After all, we should be used to this waiting game by now. Some children are whining and I hear one young mother crying. She sits across from us. Some mothers are really sick. Maybe also from sitting in the burning sun all afternoon. What can we do? Children cry, finally fall asleep. So we sit all night, half asleep, waiting for this train to move.

Finally, towards morning, I feel a shudder go through our car. Some children call out, "We're going, we're going!" We warn each other, this is it! Yes, we are moving, a rumble follows and slowly the train pulls out of Ambarawa. When it gathers speed, we all ask again, "I wonder where we are going?"

It's early in the morning. Now that we are moving the heat seems less intense and the air seems less dense, but it is still hard to breathe in this crowded, closed-up train car. Most women are stretching and yawning after a night on these hard wooden seats. Children are waking up, asking for food or drink. Some seem to be excited about the ride and no wonder, it is at least something different. But there are not many smiles. They also seem to realize that this is not a pleasure trip.

After riding for quite a while we hear the squealing of brakes and slowly our train comes to a stop. All kinds of questions and suggestions about where we are fly over and back through the car. Nobody has a clue. During our stop we feel our car bumping and stumping. Are they adding cars on to the train or are they taking some off? We wait for an interminable time while the heat is building up again. When finally the temperature seems unbearable, we go again. It seems that we have changed direction; it is just a feeling, but then I hear somebody exclaim, "Thank goodness, we are not going to Semarang [a coastal city in the north of central Java], we are going south!" I am sure that person must have peeked and noticed the direction the train took.

Mama says, "Maybe they are taking us back to Solo, maybe that's what they are supposed to do when the war comes to an end." We doubt it though, but we are full of expectations. Thus far we have heard nothing about the course this war has taken, about who is winning or losing. Judging by their erratic behavior the Japanese could be losing. Would they, would the Japs be losing? But why this closed, boarded up train? It was all so puzzling.

In the meantime we are riding on. This train is a slow boat, it just chugs on. Nobody has given us food or drink so far. Mama hands out a couple of thin slices of our dried glue bread and we each get a sip of water. I could drink a pail full. It is a little bit cooler now that we are moving. Mama says, "We don't have much water left, one more time to go. I hope we arrive soon." No comment. We are tired and defeated. I am thinking, "The seats are hard."

Several hours have gone by without stopping when suddenly we are slowing down. Are we there? Stopping can mean that we are getting off or more heat and waiting. "It's Solo, it's Solo," go the whispers. We don't dare open windows but apparently someone has recognized the station. I peek through a split bamboo window cover and happen to see a sign with the name Solo on it. I say, "It *is* Solo." It feels funny to be so close to our familiar surroundings and not to get off. We wait in the glowing heat again. It is steaming hot in the Solo valley. Children are fussing and whining, asking for water and they are shushed by their mothers. We ask for a drink of water and it helps a bit. Mama says, "That's it, just pray that we soon will be there." We have nothing to eat either. We are used to being hungry but now we have nothing to look forward to.

Again the time creeps by and we sweat and sweat. Some women and children are sick from the heat. I say to Mama, "This is inhuman! How can they do this to us?" Mama has no answer. She just strokes the heads of the little ones, who are sitting dead still at her feet.

Another train has just rumbled by ours and after it has passed, we start moving again. I guess we had to wait for a clear track to head out of Solo. Goodbye Solo, we were so close! It is almost 5:00 P.M., our time. We never changed to the new Jap time which was declared the official time for all parts of Asia when conquered by Japan. I hear a discussion between some women that we are now heading southwest, maybe Jogjakarta? But by now we don't care so much any more. Jogjakarta is approximately sixty kilometers from Solo. Another hour? The train does not go so fast, could it be another couple of hours?

It is getting darker and within minutes it is pitch dark. That is the tropical way. Night has fallen. Still no lights inside the train cars. Children are stirring and calling for food or drink, the older ones are silent, so are the adults, and the train rattles on.

At the head of our car we hear stirring and some noises. A hushed whisper makes us alert, "The Jap is coming, the Jap is at the door!" All the people stumble stiffly to their feet in the dark on this unsteady train. We have to stand and bow. If we don't, darkness or not, we're dead! We must bow when the Jap is near.

From the door through the middle aisle a dim flashlight glares into our night-blind eyes. Two guards slowly enter our car, taking their time. There is silence. No one calls, "Kiwotsuke!" Why? I am bent over, bowing anyway, so is my family and everyone else. In the dark a whisper of voices reach my ears, "It's 'Hansel my slave', it's 'Hansel my slave!'", the so-called good Jap, who took care of our boys. They are close to us now. I see vague contours of caps, uniforms, boots. Then I feel my hand being grabbed by one of them. A shiver goes through me. What now? I feel a package pushed into my hand. Then my hand is free again! No one says a thing. The Japanese men move on and leave our car. Everyone relaxes.

Mama says in the dark, "Joke, did he do something to you? What did he do, what happened?" She is scared.

"No Mama, no", I say, "he gave me something, here feel it." "A package of cigarettes!" she says astonished and then, logical as she is, "and you don't even smoke!" We all laugh.

I am just as surprised. I never had anything to do with "Hansel my slave." Ids always said that he was not the worst Jap and that his name was Kano. Later he used to bring messages over from the boys in the boys camps, but never from Ids. He used to stroll through Ambarawa 2, always smiling and he was never abusive. At one time, some ladies said that he had told them that he was a Christian and that he admired mothers with large families. Now, that is Mama. That is about all I know about the man. Maybe I can use the cigarettes to trade for food?

It sure gives me something to think about. He is the enemy. Could there be a single soul, among all the indecent, savage Japs we have experienced so far, who does not approve of all this cruelty? I'll never know. Jesus says that we should love our enemies. I am sure that nobody here on this train could do that. That is too difficult to even think about, if not impossible.

Finally the train comes to a halt. This *must* be it. I stand up. Boy oh boy, am I stiff. It must be around eight. The doors are opened and I hear them yelling already. Good for them, they have been quiet all day, so nice to be able to start again! The screaming means that we have to get out, at last. I am grappling for my *barang* in the dark, we all do. I say, "I hope that our mattresses have come along, I feel like stretching out." Mama asks if we have everything. "Don't leave anything." We feel around in the dark, there is nothing left on the benches and on the floor.

"Let's hold on to each other and stay close," Mama advises, if that is possible with our hands full, but we follow the shuffling feet towards the open doors. We are all swaying from the train ride and from hunger. We were a whole day in this dirty train without food or water! Once outside it is cooler right away. Fresh air. I fill my lungs with it and I can almost taste it. On the little station platform we can see slightly by the glow of a small light bulb that tries to penetrate into the misty night. Everybody is blinking and rubbing their eyes.

Here it is again, all these tired women and children are shouted and screamed at again. Can't these soldiers talk normally? What do they want now? "Goh, goh, goh," they scream hoarsely, "Goh, goh, goh . . . ." On and on we hear this sound, what does it mean?

Someone smart and whose brain still works, informs the crowds, "Line up five-by-five, line up five-by-five." Of course: itji, ni, san, sji, *goh*, rokoe . . . . We do it. It reminds me of the Israelites leaving Egypt the same way, "five-by-five," but for them the circumstances were somewhat different.

Mama with the little ones and Ann and Liesje line up, that's five. Emmy and I with three other persons are right behind them. Everyone catches on, we have to walk again.

We can see a tiny bit but as soon as the group starts moving we are heading into the darkest darkness. There is no moon and no stars.

Little Pete lifts his legs really high with each step he makes and Mama asks, "What are you doing Pete?"

"I am stepping in a big hole," he answers.

"There is no hole, dear," says Mama. "Just hold on to me. It is very dark but we are on the road. We are following all the others."

"I cannot see," he says again, but he does not cry and continues to make his big high steps. He could have the night blindness caused by a lack of vitamins. Many other people are scared.

I am glad that it is cooler here. We seem to be climbing steadily. It feels like we are in the mountains again. In Sumowono it was cooler at night. It's at least a soothing thought. We did not end up in the valley or some harbor town like Semarang, where the heat continues day and night.

I don't know how long this walk will be. We don't talk much as we have to concentrate on the rough road. The guards are running alongside our group. I suppose to prevent us from wandering off the road in this bitter darkness. Why is it so intensely dark? Is it an omen for our future?

I am so tired, even after sitting all night and day in that dirty train. I am carrying this heavy load again, but it seems a little better than yesterday because the sun is not blazing over us. And maybe we will soon be in the next camp. What will await us there? I am looking forward to it in a way. When we are there I can go to sleep!

The parade slows down. Now we are standing still. The people at the front of the line must have arrived. That was not too long a walk, maybe half an hour? We slowly reach the big gatehouse where we have to enter and get through to get into the camp. After being counted by the guards we are welcomed by some women. There are lights here and it feels strange to be able to see again.

The women give instructions and Mama, the little ones, Ann and Liesje are led away by another person who guides them to our new room. Emmy and I decide to wait for the trucks to arrive with our mattresses and our other *barang*. The people at the gate tell us that this camp is called Muntilan and that it lies on the steep slopes of a volcano in central Java.

Not very long afterwards the trucks come in. They must have been loaded by coolies as we had nothing to do with it this time. It is routine for us now, we find our possessions soon enough. Ann has come back to the gates to help us carry and to tell us where to go with it. With some helpful camp people we manage to get it all to our room. It is quite a distance from the gates. The camp seems to be built upon a hill. It seems to be huge but our room is so small. There are thirteen people living in it already and the room is slightly larger than a normal bedroom. With the seven of us added on, there will be twenty altogether. The people really had to move up in order to make room for us and they don't seem very happy about it.

How will this turn out? We all quenched our terrible thirst.

At least, we are here. This was some trip! The little ones are beat and so is Mama. We put our five mattresses down on the assigned spaces and fall down to sleep. Tomorrow we'll see again.

Joke Talsma, April 1946.

Papa and Mama on their wedding day, 1922

Joke, Emmy, Sietse, 1928

Sietse, Emmy, Joke, with our *kebon, baboe,* and *kokki*

Papa in front of Idenburg School with his staff

Papa comes home from school

Our home before the war, 1942

Our home after the war, 1982

Christian Reformed Church, Margojudan, Solo

My Higher Citizen School (H.B.S.), our second camp

On front verandah: Mama with Liesje and Sietse

Standing *(left to right)*: Ids, Emmy, Pete, Ann, Joke, Liesje. Seated: baby Elly.

Fourteen

Muntilan, Camp 7

OUR SEVENTH CAMP was situated on the slopes of the mountain Merapi, a twin to the Merbabu, though they are altogether different. These mountains are both in central Java. The Merapi was and still is an active volcano and columns of smoke can be seen at all times coming out of the top. The Merbabu, however, is a dormant volcano and has not erupted in ages.

The camp was called Muntilan and when we arrived there were already three thousand women and children there. With our group it became approximately thirty-eight hundred. It had been a Roman Catholic seminary, probably so secluded for the education of Roman Catholic priests. It held three hundred young men in normal times, plus teaching staff and servants.

When we woke up that first morning in our new room we were starved. But we could count on the morning blubber porridge (That is what they called it in this camp). Here also, there was nothing new under the sun! The other people in the room did not seem very friendly, at least not at first. They all came from Surabaya and were Marine people, whose husbands served with the Royal Netherlands Marines. This was their first camp and we were looked upon as intruders who took their living space away. And, we soon heard sarcastic remarks about *their* food! "With you coming in we will not get any more food and how are we going to live?" whereupon Mama replied, "We did not come here of our own free will, this is our seventh camp!" and their mouths dropped open. "What?" and then Mama gave them a short history of our experiences.

That seemed to have broken the ice and gradually in the coming weeks we were accepted. They were actually a happy bunch of people except for their language. They used swear words in practically every sentence, even the children used that kind of talk regularly. Very soon after our arrival Mama kindly asked all of them if they could watch it and it was taken surprisingly well. It helped somewhat.

There were no bunk beds for us so we spread our beds in two different spaces in the small room. We fixed up two wide beds. For one we put boards over our suitcases and baskets and put a couple of our mattresses on top. Mama was at the entrance of the room with the little ones and Liesje (four in a bed). Not the nicest spot to be in, as everyone had to pass by the open bed to get in or out of the room. But who was complaining—we came in last. Ann, Emmy, and I had the other bed on the opposite side of the room with two single mattresses flat on the floor. Our backpacks served as pillows. We put little *tikers* on top of our mattresses instead of sheets, for by now they were pretty dirty. If we wanted something out of the suitcases we had to lift up Mama's bed.

Soon we discovered how big this compound was, but it

was much cleaner than Ambarawa 2. Like Sumowono it was built terrace-wise, very widely spread out and much larger. There were bedrooms along open galleries, bathrooms, toilets over a little stream and way on the other side of the camp were toilets on septic tanks. Over there were also the study halls, classrooms, the main building for the teaching staff, a library, big campus grounds for sports, wash areas, the kitchens and, at the very back of the camp, housing for servants. On our side, quite centered was a huge, but now heavily polluted swimming pool. Most of the water used in the kitchens and our laundry came out of this swimming pool. Large grounds indeed.

The library had no books in it; actually, none of the buildings contained anything of the original seminary. Now they were filled with women and children only. The front gatehouses and the big Roman Catholic church were occupied by the Japanese and native guards. All around the whole compound were double barbed wire fences.

This camp was already very organized when our group of prisoners came in. We were integrated into this little world where in the Dutch way everything was kept as clean as possible. With so many people there, hygiene was of the essence. And even if the guards pushed everyone to work, work, work, we understood the importance of cleaning up. From age six to sixty, everyone had a particular task. Liesje had to work with the toilet group again. The guards spied on us though and if they did not find the camp clean enough or if people were not doing anything, they would let them physically feel how improvements could be made. From 6:00 sunup till 6:00 sundown we had to move. Quite often though they came roaring through camp when all the work was done and chased us all again to work, work, work.

This camp had a large hospital area and clinic. The hospital was always full. There were many sick people among the almost four-thousand prisoners. The nurses had set up a small lab where they produced different yeasts made of banana and papaya peels. Many sick women and children had to stay in their own rooms, but they could also take advantage of this service. Little six- and seven-year-old boys went around the camp galleries calling out loudly what had to be picked up, from meals to yeasts, and so forth. It was amazing how fast these children matured.

At this time of our existence our clothes were pretty well worn out and during the first weeks in this camp we were sewing, by hand, new shorts and underwear out of old skirts, drapes, and sheets. We also hemmed triangle tops, called *plastrons*, because all our blouses and tops fell apart. We still tried to remember and make birthdays somewhat special by creating a little handmade gift which brought a bit of cheer to the event. Bigger families enjoyed more variation through family life. Even in a room full of people we always supported each other. I guess single people were more involved with themselves and seemed to become sick more often.

By now all our menstrual periods had stopped. We were not the only ones. Almost all ladies and young girls discovered it and soon we learned from each other that the reason for the "no-show" was a general undernourishment. "Two weeks of better food and particularly egg whites will bring it back," said the nurses in camp. Not that we missed it, mind you, but it was unnatural. It also saved us a lot of soap.

As in all other camps the Japanese camp commander was never happy. Women and young girls did not work hard enough, said he. After an early breakfast of the glue-like tapioca porridge, on which we had to exist till noon, we had to assemble at the front gates. Emmy, Ann, and I were also summoned to work with this group of about two hundred people. We would collect *patjols*, shovels and other garden equipment and after the regular bowing ceremonies, we would walk up the dirt mountain road guarded by two to four surrogate guards.

Surrogate guards were native guards, often former members of the Royal Netherlands Indian Army. They were trained in the cruelties of the Japanese army, but they were not allowed to carry rifles or guns. They carried sticks instead, shaped like a rifle. We had a nickname for these creeps and called them the "sticks army."

This labor group existed before we came. The mountain road ended where we had to work. Strips of the jungle had to be cleared. Parts were so dense they had to be hacked clean. After that was done we cleared roots and rocks out of the stretch. Then we shoveled and dug until the ground and soil was smooth enough to plant gardens for vegetables; spinach, cabbage, carrots, and so forth. but we were never allowed to harvest any of it.

The commander was always telling us that high officers would arrive soon, to inspect the fields and the fields should show how hard the women had learned to work, instead of being lazy as they had been before. So the spinach shot up into seed, so did the cabbage, and everything else rotted away when the rains fell and burnt up when it was too dry. And this went on and on. If we didn't work hard enough we were yelled at. You just did what you were told or else a beating would follow.

As we were very hungry at this time of our imprisonment, we certainly tried to smuggle in some of the leafy veggies inside of our blouses or plastrons. But one day a girl accidentally dropped something and the punishment was drastic.

This is how we were all punished: At the gate house we all had to stand opposite each other and then we were ordered to beat each other up. This sounds funny, but it was not. If we giggled or did not beat hard enough, the screaming soldiers or the guards would do it for us, so we beat. Just in case it would happen again we prepared each other not to beat so hard, but just to pretend. That did not always work though, as some girls panicked and really hit hard. It was horrifying. Emmy came home once on a rainy day when, for one reason or other, the whole group of women and girls had been punished by the guards in this terrible, inhumane way. She was bruised all over. We warned each other after that not to smuggle any more, to avoid any repeat beatings. It was not worth it.

But we became very inventive because we were hungry. Occasionally we smuggled in some salad leaves in our underpants in order to have a bit of a richer water soup at supper even if the produce was somewhat wilted!

A couple of months later another group of prisoners entered this camp. We were surprised to find Bertha Harwig among them with Jan and Jopie. She had been taken to Solo first and now again she was moved to Muntilan. It was apparent that that had been the reason for our long delay in Solo, as a group of prisoners had been dropped off. It was all so senseless!

My garden chores were interrupted at one time because I was asked to help out a family whose mother had become sick. She was the wife of the minister who had lent his car to Papa at the time when he needed it. Mrs. Kuiper went into the camp hospital, completely exhausted. There were four children to tend. The baby stayed with a neighbor in the room and I took care of the other three children plus the complete household and it was hectic! They were busy children who did not want to eat the poor camp food. That was the biggest chore, to get them to eat. After two weeks I fainted while doing their laundry. The children at that time were visiting their mother in the relaxation room of the hospital. That was it, I could not do it any more. I had been running around with hunger edema for a while already, but I had thought that this job would be easier than working in the fields. It was a different kind of stress. I myself was now exhausted, practically no food, busy days and nights, it was too much! Mrs. Kuiper came back to her room and I had to take a week off. But when the week was up, I was called again to work outside the camp. No rest for the wicked . . . .

There was another group of approximately thirty girls who had to work outside the campgrounds. They were the ones who carried human manure. Sounds strange? Well, this explains it: The septic tanks were completely overloaded and failing with such an overpopulation. They were actually constantly overflowing. The stench was unbearable and the danger of increasing infections was acute. Our women camp leaders constantly complained to the camp commander, "So many women and children in such a cramped area, is it a wonder that things go wrong?"

The man said, "Empty them . . ."

Our camp-leaders asked, "How . . . ?"

"Scoop it out," said he.

That's how this particular chore was created. We were supplied with buckets, the lids of the septic tanks were re-moved and the contents were scooped out. Then these buckets with the smelly, contagious guck in them were carried between two girls to the garden fields and dumped in the trenches alongside the plants. If you or your partner stumbled or tripped, the goo would spill on your legs and there was no way of getting it off until you were back in camp. This was an ongoing job. Upon our return the tanks had already filled up again.

Emmy and I put in our names for this group mainly to give ourselves a break from working the fields. After my little side job, we were called up. With so many sick and weak people, there always was a big turnover of workers. Every day there were different girls with us. We were called the *stront ploeg,* the shit gang. Emmy and I acted as if we had done this work forever.

We became very tough but I guess not as tough as some of the head girls, Jo and Lien, of this gang. If, for instance, some of the new girls acted too sissy about the dirt or if they complained too much about the smell, they would "accidentally" be pushed into the hole of the tank. They were fished out again, of course, but Jo and Lien would calmly say, "See if they come back, we don't need suckers!" Most of the time the girls would come back, as there was more variety in this job. Even if we walked barefooted all day long on an empty stomach in the hot glaring sun, the humor of these young girls kept us going.

As Jo and Lien always had to be up front with the Japanese guards and being in a leading position, they took bigger chances. They tried to introduce our Dutch humor to them, which seldom worked and they got slapped around for it. But at one time they started calling the Jap Haiassi, Donald Duck. He really looked like a duck with his bowlegs and he certainly waddled like one. We had a hard time keeping straight faces, but to everyone's surprise, he liked it and laughed about it. He even insisted on being called that way as if he was proud of it. Strange man.

At times we would meet other young people on the road who were taking a tub of hot sweetened tea to the *patjollers* (the shovel group). We were forbidden to talk with each other, but we would pretend not to know them and whisper questions like this, "Which camp are you from?" They would catch on and answer, "Oh, we're from far away, we have walked all day. Where are you from?" We would answer again that we were from Muntilan and so on and then we would whisper our good-byes when we passed each other. These were the only little breaks in our dull existence.

At night when we were back at our room we could barely move. We had to drag ourselves to the *mandi*-room. Luckily there always seemed to be enough cold water in the *mandi* basin. It sure helped to get cleaned up but it was a big effort to get our body there as our spirit was numb by that time. After a meager supper usually of a thin watery soup made up of whatever the cooks still could find, we dropped on our sleeping mats and slept. There are many more stories about this camp.

Fifteen

Muntilan, Camp 7
More Stories

AGAIN THE Japanese camp commander declared that we didn't work hard enough and that we slept too much. Besides that, he decided it was not safe enough in camp even if double barbed wire surrounded us! Anyway, we had to walk an extra hour in the night watch. He called it *fu sin bang.*

This night watch had started in all camps in Ambarawa and it had been a nuisance over there. We had not been involved as much in camp Ambarawa 2, but now it had to be three hours long. Nine o'clock at night was lights out, so we had to walk from nine to midnight, from midnight to 3:00 A.M., from 3:00 to 6:00 A.M. Each block had to bring up the required women or girls, two for each shift. The "sticks army" guards would come around to check on all the watch runners and we never knew when. Occasionally the Japanese commandant would be with them.

Tired, hungry, and full of edema as we were, it had to be done. I'll take my sister Emmy as an example of our general appearance. She was eighteen years old in this camp, five feet ten inches tall and at that time she weighed seventy-nine pounds, that is short of forty kilograms. She was *vel over been* (skin on bones). She was drying up. Little children had run into her protruding hipbones and had come up crying while a big lump developed on their heads. Her thighs were like sticks and were thinner than her legs. I myself had the kind of beriberi which retains fluids in the body and I looked all puffed up, an awful feeling!

We were on our feet the whole day doing hard labor. It was no wonder that this interrupted night rest hit hard. We tried to get as many ladies as possible to take their turns, but most of them were sick or too weak. It seemed that our turns came up more and more often!

We were not allowed to talk, which we did anyway, to sit down, which could mean bloodshed, or even to stand still. We slowly strolled up and down the open galleries alongside the rooms of our block. Lengthy blocks of buildings were constructed on the slope of the mountain as if they were sitting on terraces, with steps in between. On particular bright moonlit nights we occasionally waved at the other watch walkers up or down from our block. Our fear was that our camp commander would come to check on us on one of those bright nights, as he was "moonstruck" and could be very cruel when he was in that mood. The guards could pop up in the dark at any moment.

This particular watch that Emmy and I were walking had gone by uneventfully. Our shift was from 3:00 to 6:00 A.M. and it was close to 6:00, still dark but daylight was slightly shimmering through. The cord on Emmy's slipper had come undone so she quickly sat down on a wooden bench on the *emper* to fasten it. I was so tired and I was just bending down to sit beside her when on the steps coming from the lower block we heard the stomping of the guards' boots. There were two guards from the "sticks army."

We rushed towards them as we were supposed to do, bowed deeply and said our message, "Dai sanpang to dai sipang, fukumudju idju arimassin" (Everything on block 3 and 4 in order). But this time they did not pay attention to our patter. One of the two asked in Malay, "Why were you sitting down?" Emmy answered in her best Malay that she had to fasten the cord on her slipper. Then he turned to me and said, "And you too?" Then suddenly his leg shot out and he kicked at both of us and stepped on top of our feet. We hastily drew back to let them pass but the other one put his fist out and let it come down on Emmy's stomach. She bent backwards, almost folded double but then caught herself on a little washline and accidentally pushed over a metal pail, which made a heck of a noise in the still morning. I guess the noise of the rolling pail changed their mind about beating us up some more.

Lots of people woke up with a shock and started peering out of the windows of their rooms to see what all the commotion was about. But we had to show the guards up to the next block and they were walking already. Hastily we rushed after the two morons and caught up just in time to say our lesson, "Susu itai fukumu ita imas" (we pass you on to the next block). Still shaking, we dragged our tired, sore feet back to our room. It was 6:00 anyway and Mama and the others stood at the door waiting to hear our story. Emmy said that by bending backwards he had not hurt her badly but of course we were humiliated. We could count ourselves lucky that it had not been the "moonstruck" Jap. Above all, within an hour we had to be on the road with the *patjol* group to go to the fields and face these jerks again. That was not a very happy morning.

At the same time of the extended *fu sin bang* we had to start the morning exercises again but luckily not for long. It sort of petered out and stopped. But skirmishes went on continually all through camp. The Japanese guards and the "sticks army" became more and more impatient. They were totally without any sense of humor. All of a sudden the order came to shave the hair off all little boys, eight years and up. That was not funny! Most Japs were shaved bald. We thought it was just pestering and it was a ridiculous thing to do.

Once the Japanese guard, nicknamed "Hansel my slave" came into camp. He was stormed by a lot of women from our former camp, Ambarawa 2, and questioned about the boys. That was a dumb thing to do. He acted very aloof and the women were very disappointed. No wonder, they could have betrayed him for smuggling notes into camp and apparently he had to protect himself, that's how we saw it. We never heard if he had notes with him on that occasion.

We were so tired and without energy that at times we could not even think straight. Several people went off their rocker, so to say. A few women got into a fist fight, forgetting where they were. Of course the commander heard about it and one of them, regardless of who was at fault, received such a beating from the man himself that after a lock up in a shed, she walked around for days with severe bruises and cuts on her body. One of the women was separated from the other and put in a little *gudang* by herself. I don't know if she liked that or not, but if someone behaved strangely in camp, people would say, "Maybe you need a little room by yourself!"

It was unnatural to live so close together for such a long time. Differences between families existed, and you just had to learn to be tactful. Sometimes families changed rooms because the daily disagreements could not be overcome. We learned a lot that way. But the malicious behavior of the Japanese aggravated these scenes. All the more reason to suspect that something was not right on their side of the war. Would we still have a chance to come out of it?

Most camp people had one good hobby or what came to be almost an addiction. That was the recipe collection. We were involved with it too. When we heard about a new delicious recipe, we *had* to have it. It was like a fever. We would find out in which room the person lived and we would go to a pure stranger to take down the tasty fantasy in our notebook. Then we would sit together to sum up all the ingredients and "eat" the finished dish over and over again in our mind. We had a whole notebook full of them, which sadly was lost in later moves. The value of food would stay with us forever. Not so much the quantity of it but the realization of it and the thankfulness for it. I still hate to waste food.

Once, in those anxious days, it happened that I headed for the kitchens to get some ashes to make soda suds for our laundry, when I heard loud screams and moans coming from inside the big Roman Catholic church. The kitchens were close to the church and the whole kitchen staff appeared quiet and tense. They told me that a young girl was being tortured. I heard later that she had received a postcard by way of the Red Cross from her mother who was a native Javanese and lived outside the camp. There had been a birth date on the card, this girl's birthday and congratulations. As everything was censored she had been called to the church where the Jap had questioned her about this date on the card. She only knew it to be her birthday and she had tried to make that clear.

Instead, she was beaten and questioned over and over about the meaning of the date. She did not know anything else. Then they had hammered bamboo pins under her nails to make her confess. To what? The rest of the day she had to sit in a kneeling position with a bamboo rod behind her knees which cut off the whole blood circulation in her legs. During that time she was kicked and beaten continuously. After a couple of hours she was made to stand up which is excruciatingly painful when the circulation starts to restore itself through the veins.

At last she ended up in our little hospital completely wasted, the poor girl. We all suggested that the girl's crucial date had something to do with a battle where the Japs suffered great losses. We learned later that, in the first months of 1945, a lot of battles *were* fought.

There were some ladies, though, who knew more about the ongoing war. One such a woman was in our room. Once in a blue moon, she used to go and play bridge, so called. We would watch her two children for her and she usually returned very late at night. The following morning she was always very cheerful and upon our questions of, "Mrs. Zomer, what did you hear last night?" she would just smile or sometimes sing, "It'll only be a few more 'poopy' days and we'll leave this rotten camp!" (which is from a Dutch song: *En het duurt nog maar een poepie dagen, en dan gaan we de rotzooi uit!*). We would all laugh but she'd never say more. Rumor had it that a group of women would assemble the different parts of a radio and listen in to the latest war news. It was possible, but nobody had anything like radios, wires, or parts in her possession any more after all the house searches we had had.

As the weeks and months crept by it seemed our food rations could not get any worse but they did! For a certain period of time we each received a small unleavened loaf of bread again, the size of a squared off bun, the same kind as we had had in Ambarawa. It was still as hard and stiff as dried up glue. Again we used to cut the thinnest slices from it to make the "bread" last longer. A lot of people could not digest this kind of starch. They either brought it up or became constipated or had diarrhea. Maybe it was a blessing when that unhealthy "bread" did not come in any more.

We also hauled in bags and bags of hard kernel corn which never got soft no matter how long you boiled it. This corn was one ingredient in our daily mixed soup. It caused many stomach ailments as nobody could digest it. Most children and lots of women developed diarrhea and the whole kernels would come out again. We chewed and chewed our soup, it was ridiculous. But then, our one ladle of soup would last somewhat longer.

In the rainy season there happened to be a lot of garden slugs or snails around. The doctors had told us that our diet totally lacked protein and slugs were pure protein. So there was a big hunt on for these slippery creatures. The cooks in the kitchens prepared a spicy *sambal* from them and at one supper there was an additional snail dish, approximately one slimy teaspoonful per person. Hungry as I was, I did not touch the glassy substance, I just could *not* eat it.

The little ones stopped asking for food also. Even at their young age, they realized it was not to be had. Once after a meal, Peter and Elly were sitting all washed and cleaned up waiting to be tucked in for bed. Their skinny little bodies with the big blue eyes in their small faces cramped up your heart. While sucking his thumb Peter said, "Mama, that was a nice dinner eh . . . ?"

Mama answered, "Yes, it was."

Peter again, "Would you like to have had a little more?"

"Yes, sure I would," said Mama again and then Pete, "But there isn't any more eh?"

Mama, "No, not now, but maybe tomorrow . . ." and she just hugged him.

Imagine, not to be able to give your little ones, and big ones, enough to eat and then also to know, that whatever they had to eat, was not good for them! How Mama and all the other mothers must have suffered over this cruel fact, that purposely their children were being starved to death. How any human being can bestow such a lot onto another human is still beyond me.

Children were dying, normal teenagers were dying. They were dying hungry. One sixteen-year-old girl who worked in the *patjol* group with us died also. She had been completely without energy. Our gym teacher's mother was asked on her deathbed if she still had one wish that maybe her daughter could fulfill for her. She asked for a soft-boiled egg and there was not one single egg to be found in the whole big camp. There also were no mice, no rats, no frogs, no grasshoppers, no earthworms, anything that possibly could be eaten was not there!

Still the slave labor went on. We stood barefooted in compost and garbage heaps to move them from one place to another. The stench in the tropical heat was suffocating. One time we had to empty a pond in the front of the camp grounds. A few native coolies had drained the dirty water until they reached the black murky layer. That part was saved for the women. They had to stomp around in their bare feet and feel with their hands to search the bottom of the pond and "find anything of value," so they were told by the Japanese camp commander. He probably suspected that the women had thrown their money and other valuables in the pond when the order came to hand everything in.

Well, he did not get much out of it. Silver spoons, jewelry, silver guilders, whatever the women found, was quickly passed on to the assisting women who were standing near the edge of the pond and had to carry the thick mud away. Everything was covered with sludge anyway, so practically nothing was handed over to him. He was visibly disappointed. All in all, it was a stinking job. Anything was done to humiliate us and to take our spirit away. A Japanese camp commander once admitted to one of our camp leaders that if they had to fight the women, they never would have won the war. At that time it seemed that Japan had won the war. She could not tell the man otherwise or else she would have received a beating. Besides, she did not know how the war would end! We never showed it, but at this stage of our existence, we were pretty low.

By the middle of 1945, the guards gave up on the gardens. They had deteriorated anyway as so many women and young people were weak and could not work a full day any more. Chores inside the camp became more difficult to finish. Mama had her duties in the kitchen and as we girls always worked outside camp she took care of our laundry and of the cleaning of our own spaces in the room. Now the camp commander said, "You all have to work much harder. There are still strong women here. I want to see them here tomorrow morning, as many as possible!"

So that next day after a call through all the blocks for

the strongest women, a large group of mostly young people stood in line for the regular puppet show. That was, *Kiwotsuke, keirei,* and *naore.* Emmy and I were also with this group. We did not know what we had to do yet.

We started marching down another mountain path winding into a large ravine. When the volcano Merapi erupted this ravine was one of the hot lava catchers. It was dry and very rocky with the biggest boulders strewn around. There we were told to start working. We had to smash the larger rocks with another rock so that they would crumble into stones. Then we had to throw these stones on a big heap. All day long in the humid heat we slaved on this job and we had no energy. Our hands were blistered and raw. We took pieces of old cloth to hold on to the rocks which we used to hammer down on the larger rocks and tried to avoid infections. Quite a few fingers were crushed in the process.

The guards stood there all day watching us. This was the worst of all our labor. This kind of work took so much out of us, it took our courage away. Occasionally the Jap Haiassi came personally to make sure we were busy and he stood there with this tiny conceited expression on his round moon face. That made our blood boil! We had to continue but it served no purpose. How they must have hated us!

When we returned late in the afternoon we were exhausted and had nothing to say or to tell any more. The days seemed so purposeless. We did not even think about our precious youth anymore which had been stolen from us. Mama was a great support when she steered us to the *mandi*-rooms to wash the dust and dirt off our shaky bodies. Then after our meager supper we always prayed together that, maybe, maybe, relief was on the way. These prayers seemed to be the only reason to go on.

Although this torture lasted only a few weeks it thoroughly wore us out. It was hard, hard labor and at this stage of our life, devastating. All of a sudden it was cancelled. When it stopped we got another huge house search out of it. We had to stand in the sun again. Then a whole army of little Japanese soldiers invaded our rooms and disrupted everything. They searched and searched in all nooks and crannies and made a complete mess again in the rooms.

Suddenly Mama was called. We had nothing of value in our room. One of us was wearing the "pants" and that was all we had to be worried about. Mama left and if the sun had been hot before, it became hotter and hotter. Our roommates asked, "What do you think it could be? Have you held something back?" I answered, "No, there is nothing I can think of among our possessions in the room. I am just as puzzled." It was not very long when Mama came back with a slight smile on her lips. "I'm all right," she said when she noticed our anxious faces. "They found our ruler and it had the abbreviation D.V.O. on it, which means Department of Education (*Onderwys* in Dutch). But it could also mean Department of War (*Oorlog* in Dutch)." She told us that the Japanese officer had been calm and quite reasonable when Mama explained and had taken her word for it, but he had taken the ruler anyway. And then she was allowed to go. We breathed a big sigh of relief. We had visions of a beaten up, bloody mother and she certainly did not deserve such a thing. It became a long hot day in the burning sun and afterwards we had to clean up the total havoc they had left. Nobody missed anything. We did not have anything anymore. These searches were so useless.

By now most of us had pellagra on top of our different kinds of beriberi. This severe lack of vitamins shows up at first on hands and feet as flaming red spots. Steadily these spots would spread and creep up higher and higher according to the severity of the vitamin deficiency. Besides these symptoms, which are very painful especially when the hot sun burns on them, people became lethargic, nothing mattered anymore and sometimes we walked around like zombies.

So it was no wonder that when we received word of another move shortly after the last search, we did not react much. We had been in Muntilan for a good six months. It was the middle of July, 1945. Time to pack up again, say good-bye to people and friends we would never see again. We never saw the women and children in our room again.

A move was always a split of groups, though we certainly had no energy to form plots against the Japanese. The same orders were handed out, we could only bring what we could carry, but mattresses were allowed. This time a group of young girls went with the trucks to the train station to load the *barang* in the train. We noticed that there actually were quite a few heavy trunks among the luggage. No coolies this time to do the heavy work. Emmy and I also worked like horses to load everything in the freight cars. We knew how disappointing it was when on arrival in the other camp, something was missing. We threw our baskets also in the train, we knew we would not have the strength to carry them again. Mama said, "Whatever we keep with us should be what we will need immediately, and we will see again when we are there." Where?

We left Muntilan on trucks. They took us to the same little station where we had arrived in January of this year. We boarded the train which we girls had loaded earlier in the day. One Japanese officer pushed Mama onto the train. There was no delay this time though. This train started to climb a steep mountain. We realized that this was the only traction railway on Java. Within a short time we ended up in the same place, Ambarawa, which we had left when we had been riding for a whole day to get to Muntilan. What a revelation! Our trip of almost twenty-four hours could have been made in about half an hour! What devilish planning.

However, *our* destination was not Ambarawa. Part of the train load went there. We had to go to Banjubiru, higher up in the mountains. And we had to walk again. A large group of people started climbing a steadily winding road for about four or five kilometers. We carried our personal backpacks and important necessary luggage and we were so tired. Ann had hepatitis and could barely move. Although it was hot she had the shivers. She wore a short sweater-jacket, which made her sweat profusely. We literally had to push her. It was just as if she did not even know she was with us. We were so worried about her.

The little ones kept asking, "Are we there Mama, are we there?" Mama had her hands full with them and with Ann. Emmy, Liesje, and I carried practically everything, also to relieve Mama and Ann. We were a slow moving group and the walk lasted quite a while. Strangely enough there were no guards to push us!

Then some trucks came up behind us. We stepped aside to let them pass on the narrow road. It was the luggage off the train, luckily they brought it along. As of now I still don't know how the luggage was ever sorted out to go to the different camps. No trucks for us though. Slowly we finally made it into the next camp.

Sixteen

Banjubiru, Camp 8 and Freedom?

WE ARRIVED at Banjubiri completely exhausted. Ann was more dead than alive. But to our surprise we discovered that for the first time in years we were going to be in a house, even if it was only on the front verandah.

This house was one of twelve old officers' houses built back to back in two rows of six. We ended up in the first house of a row of six, facing away from the rising jungle on the mountains which rose steeply right behind our camp. Later on this proved to be to our advantage. The front verandah was not too bad. We had two double bunk beds and luckily our four remaining mattresses had come along with the trucks. They were pretty dirty by now but it was still better than sleeping on the floor or on boards. It was pretty narrow though, with two persons per single bed. Again, this camp was surrounded by some barbed wire and some shabby looking *gedek*. Our house was close to the gate, but we did not care any more. We could not change it anyway.

My first memories of this camp are vague, especially of the first weeks. Probably because I was so tired everything happened in a daze. Our slave labor in Muntilan, the poor, insufficient meals, the anxiety about another move and the hardships of it, all piled up and seemed to have defeated us temporarily.

After a couple of days we started to recover. At least, there was no group labor outside the camp. Meals were not too bad and not too skimpy. We received cooked rice for the first time in months! The people already there were friendly and we recognized quite a few from our former camp Ambarawa 2. They had been shipped here when that camp had been emptied. And also, there were hardly any Japanese soldiers around. Our guards were *heihos*, but they stayed out of our way and sat mainly at the front gate. What was going on?

Soon enough we were involved with camp chores. We discovered that one of the houses was solely used as a hospital and it was full of sick, worn-out women. There was a lot of help needed. We girls spent a few days on hospital duties, cleaning up and supplying food to the sick. The food had to be picked up from the central kitchen. Most patients were too weak to eat unless they were assisted.

We discovered the "fat lady" in the hospital, Mrs. Laarman, who used to be our next bed neighbor in Ambarawa 2. She also had been moved to this camp. The lady was completely drained of all her energy. This happened more often with mothers who gave their food to their kids. Or, as appeared to be the case with this lady, who had sold all her food, meager as it was, for cigarettes. Nothing is nothing, you cannot live on that.

She had lost all her weight too fast and now was skin and bone. Her skin was doubled up in layers against her body. There had been no time for the skin to shrink normally and when she was bathed, the layers had to be lifted up in order to clean underneath. And still, weak as she was, her sense of humor prevailed. "Soon," she said when she saw us, "we will go out and treat ourselves to cake and ice cream again." She remembered! That was the Dutch spirit that kept us alive.

Being in the mountains again was in our favor. The air was cooler at night. Only at our arrival had there been some Japanese around. It was very strange that in the following weeks, we did not see any at all nearby. We only had one or two guards at the gates who left us alone. There was a quiet hush over this camp. All the worn out people kept to themselves.

It made us think, if Japan had won the war, they would want the Dutch out of this country and the only way to do that was to send them back to Holland. But if Japan had lost the war or was losing it, they would either kill us or treat us with kid gloves. But actually nothing was going on. Why no forced labor, why no Japanese checking up, why the minimum of guards?

Was something happening out there? Was it almost over? So many questions, no answers, we heard nothing! There were also no encouraging signs of any sort. Even if there was more rice around, the meals still were so insufficient and poor that we were just miserable and hunger was aching in our bodies.

Practically everyone in the camp population was running around with an edema of some kind, either the puffiness or the drying out one. I did not want to think about the frightening results of pellagra, the deficiency that caused the fiery red blotches on hands, feet, and legs. Mine had crept up past my ankles already. I banned the effects of this fatal disease out of my mind, the higher it crept the closer to death! But the pain was always there, day and night, as a reminder. The nurses said, "The only way to get rid of it is better food!" We did not have it.

Mama and the little ones also kept quiet. If there were any chores required of Mama, we older girls tried to relieve her. We had done that in Muntilan but now it seemed more necessary. As young people, we did not have much energy either, but we wanted our Mama to survive. She had lost so much weight and had turned into a small little woman, so different from what she had been before. As a family we were so protective of each other.

Room had come available and we were able to move inside the house. We had a whole living room to ourselves by now. This was more private and also dryer in case of the rains. Ann had miraculously recovered from her hepatitis and looked more cheerful. But now Mama had developed a sore on her ankle and it did not heal so the nurse in the clinic had advised her to rest. We helped as much as possible but it worried us. Liesje looked puffy too.

We had been about a month in this camp and it was around the 22nd or 23rd of August when we were all called to assemble on a small lawn between some of the houses. The call was made by our camp leader. Mama could not go and she was not interested either. We all went to see what was up. Most women and children came and while we were waiting, some general questions arose, "What now? Where are the guards? No Japanese soldiers? Do you know why we are here?"

A hush fell over the crowd when our camp leader stepped forward. She did not let us wait long. She spoke, "The war is over, Japan has lost, we are free . . . . On the 15th of August they capitulated to the Allied Forces." That was the message. We were silent.

Then someone started our National Anthem, the "Wilhelmus van Nassaue," and we sang, trembling. There was no Dutch flag but it did not matter. Then we cheered, we laughed, we cried, we kissed, we believed it! Finally it was over, we were free, and we listened to the rest of the story.

Apparently a bomb had been dropped on Japan with terrible but terrific results. What the terrible part was, nobody knew. The terrific part was that Japan had surrendered! Everyone smiled. We ran home to tell Mama. The children played a little harder. We all appeared to have a burst of energy and courage. The ladies were advised to stay in camp until our friends, the liberators, would arrive, whoever they might be.

The next morning a couple of native policemen were sitting at the gates instead of the sticks army guards and the gates stood wide open . . . . Some brave ladies prepared to leave the camp anyway. "We want to get our boys," they said. "They are still in Ambarawa and it is only a few kilometers from here. We'll bring our sons home!" As our house was close to the gates, we saw them leave and we saw them return with their boys! They informed us that all our boys were in camp Ambarawa 2, now called Camp 7, the camp we had left before we went to Muntilan.

Mama said, "We should get Ids too," and that was exactly what we girls had in mind. Mama still had to sit with her leg and Emmy had kitchen duties. That's why Ann and I set out early the next morning. We were accompanied by many other mothers and sisters whose boys had been taken away. Our spirits were high and we experienced a new willpower. There was something to talk about and to hope for. Our lives had not ended, we were not alone and we knew in which camp Ids was.

The walk down the mountain road was so different. We were in Ambarawa in no time at all. Some of the women knew their way around in the small town and guided us all. The gates of the boys' camp stood wide open. I remembered the high wooden gates. Some smaller boys were playing around the entrance. When we entered the camp, a voice called out, "Ann, Ids is in that barrack." We looked up and recognized the boy as Harry, the son of one of our neighbors in Solo. He was the brother of my best girlfriend Els and he had been in the same grade in school as Ann.

After greetings of surprise, Harry led us into the barrack he had pointed out. All different sizes of boys were sitting or lying around on the bunk beds. Some were even sitting in the rafters. Harry shouted, "Ids, look who is here?" Ids turned around and saw us. He said, "Hi, how did *you* get here?" We answered, "We walked . . ." and then we grabbed him and we hugged and patted him on the back. We were all smiles. We sat down on his bunk and exchanged information about our whereabouts and about being free. Ids told some incredible stories of his stay in this camp and he told us too that he was just recovering from a very severe camp fever. He had not expected us yet, but we told him we had come to take him with us.

Some other boys volunteered more of their experiences and we learned how harsh their existence had been. Most of the boys looked dirty and tired but their spirit was good. They said they were waiting for their moms to pick them up. We also saw a lot of edema.

After a while we asked Ids if he could leave and if he had to tell someone. He said, "You have to have something to eat first. We have lots!" We had noticed the live chickens and ducks already, tied to the different bedposts. The boys had been trading with the natives by exchanging old socks, pants, even old cloths for food. They dished up cold chicken, fish, rice with *sayur* and fruit; we could take as much as we wanted.

While we were eating the boys told us that the native population had mainly been asking for clothing and had been the ones to come to the fences with food to trade. Apparently the Japanese occupancy of the country had also deprived them of practically everything. They had taken away their most normal way of living. Their lives had been peaceful and secure. The occupation forces had ordered them to hand in a large part of their hard-earned income. The products of their labor had been shipped out of the country, destination Japan! The native population had not been able to buy any kind of clothing all these years. By trading food the people tried to get their hands on something that at least looked like cloth. The boys' barrack was a mess. In order to find cloth for trading they had ripped some mattresses apart and the *kapok* (stuffing) was flying everywhere, but they did not care.

Now the boys were eating. They had also been starved in their camp. They were so proud to be able to offer us something. We had talked about overeating after the war, and the possible consequences of making ourselves sick, but it was so good to eat!

We told Ids that Mama was so anxious to see him again and also that we had heard nothing from Papa yet. Ids had matured so much and he knew what to do. He told us to wait while he said good-bye to all his friends. He packed up his little bundle and his backpack while we said good-bye to

Harry and wished him a welcome home. He did not know yet where his family was. We heard later that they had been taken to Semarang.

Then we were out of there. We walked and walked. I cannot remember how soon we made it back to Banjubiru. I only know how happy we were to have Ids with us. Mama cried and hugged and held him. She commented how well he looked, whereupon Ids sarcastically answered, "Yes, this is real wartime chubbiness!" We understood that he meant that he also had hunger edema. It was true, he was all puffed up in his face, ankles and legs. Then we too made plans to start trading for food.

Luckily our camp people had started the exciting game that same day, slowly at first, later openly trading with the natives through the *gedek*. We searched through the few clothes we could spare and traded for extra rice and fruit. But soon trucks came by and brought more food for the kitchen so that the staff could prepare better meals for the whole camp.

Ids was a pro at trading and on one of those days he came up with a live duck. The little ones thought it was so cute but when Ids slaughtered it, little Pete promptly vomited, poor fellow. He was still so innocent. We had a delicious meal with all the extra meat, but we were careful not to overeat, as duck is quite greasy.

Ids easily settled in with us again. We were so happy he had been close enough to find so soon. Mama tried to put a little bit of regular living back to our family life. We were eating our meals together again and at our family devotions we always thanked the Lord that the war was over and hoped that maybe we would get word from Papa soon.

Meanwhile, weeks went by and the only guards at the

gates were the same old native policemen, who were friendly enough, but where were our liberators, soldiers, navy men, air force? Rumor had it that the Japs of our camps had been strung up upside down by the native rebels, but I cannot confirm this. There were lots of speculations, guesses, but we realized that there were no liberation troops covering the women's camps.

Some airplanes came over once in a while to drop food packs, but we did not get much from it. We were at such an outpost. I suppose it was mainly medicine. Sometimes we walked outside the camp just for the feeling of being free. We were waiting for something to happen.

Once, a truck came by with a bag of mail. We also received a letter. Mama cried out when she recognized the handwriting, "It is from Papa, it is from Papa," she exclaimed, "and I am not sure, it says: L. and S. Talsma. Could it be that they are together? The letter is from Singapore!" She opened it while we all stood around her. We knew now that Papa was alive, however not well. He had found Sietse, who had come out from Holland to the Far East in order to help liberate the Indies. "If you have a chance, you should come to Singapore. We will be waiting," Papa wrote. And . . . there was a picture with the letter, as proof that they were together. We were so happy. Our whole family, all ten of us, survived, thank the Lord!

Towards the end of September, 1945, a couple of huge tanks suddenly drove up the road and stopped alongside the camp fences. On top of them sat a few Indian soldiers in battle dress, with turbans on their heads. They were the Sikhs. The liberators had finally made it and had come to protect our camps. We were so excited! This could mean that we would soon be out of the camp.

But, the first night some girls in our camp were almost assaulted by these guys! Nobody was safe from them. They were crazy about anything that just slightly looked like a female. Our camp leader had to request a replacement for this team of maniacs. It was granted and in their place fourteen Gurkhas arrived, little men whose home country was Nepal, near the Himalayas. They spoke broken English and they were the friendliest men we had encountered in a long time. They camped in one of the first houses on the side of the mountain. These men were the perfect soldiers. They were dedicated, stood on guard day and night. They had everything with them, from the heaviest artillery to the tiniest cooking pot. We felt safe but we wondered about the tight watch schedules. Did they know something we didn't? We would soon find out!

Not very long after their arrival snipers started shooting bullets into our camp from high up in the mountains behind us. Our camp was an easy target. But they were such bad shots nobody got hurt. Of course we panicked. The guard was doubled and we were told to keep under the protection of the buildings when we had to be outside. Now being away from the mountain side proved to be to our advantage as we were safer from the attacks. Sometimes we really had to hide as the bullets rattled on the roof, but this came in spurts. The shootings were erratic at first and at night it was usually calm. Even so, it was a rotten feeling. Was this freedom?

The camp leaders informed us that the snipers were guerrilla fighters, rebels against the former Dutch government. They called themselves *merdeka* (independence) fighters. All the Japanese weapons and stocks were now in their hands and they had started attacks with a vengeance against all

Dutch people, beginning with the women's camps, the cowards! We were completely helpless and almost starved to death. We had nothing to defend ourselves with, except now fourteen Gurkhas.

At night some of the soldiers who were off duty came over to our house with large cans of cheese, corned beef, salmon, butter, and fruit. They said that a big family needed "big" food. We accepted it all gratefully and they seemed to enjoy family closeness. One Gurkha, who called himself Chris, was one of our regular visitors. He was always kind and smiling and never forgot to bring a surprise. Even Mama was affected by his charms and she often said, "That Chris fellow is such a friendly man." They all had pictures of their families with them and we were invited to come and visit them some day in their country.

Several families had left our camp when their husbands and fathers had come back. So it happened that our family was the only occupant of our house. We had nothing to furnish it with, so we only kept two adjacent rooms, one for sleeping, one for living. The rest of the house was used at night for the recreation and entertainment of mostly young people. There happened to be an old piano in the big dining room which was in pretty good tune.

One of the girls played the boogie-woogie on the piano while the whole gang of teenagers danced to the music. It was so much fun! The Gurkha soldiers stood at the doors watching us. We realized how much we had been deprived of pleasures during the last four years. Some older boys had also come back from the P.O.W. camps to find their families and we noticed the son of our doctor in Solo among them. His mom and sister were with us in Banjubiru. Usually the kids left for their "camp" homes before ten o'clock and the noise never bothered us. Everyone was still pretty worn out but we needed this recreation.

It had been weeks since the liberation, which, we had learned, was announced to us about ten days late. The official date had been August 15, 1945. Now, at the end of September, we also learned that the first Allied warships had only entered the harbor of Tandjong Priok near Batavia on the 16th of September, late enough for us all to have been slaughtered by the guerrilla fighters. This had actually happened to a group of Marine women and children who had returned to Surabaya. They had all been tortured and killed, a terrible occurrence after having survived the women's camps. We were thinking of our roommates in Muntilan. They had all been from Surabaya! Could they have been among them?

By October the attacks from the mountains behind our camp became more frequent, even regular! One of our Gurkhas was killed. This infuriated the others and us also. We had become such friends in those couple of weeks. From then on the Gurkhas shot at anything that moved up in the mountains. Even a boy guiding his goats was shot down. We were advised not to leave the camp at all, not to show ourselves outside except under cover of the buildings. And it became worse.

There was serious talk that we had to get out of there before anything more dreadful could happen. And yes, our liberators, the British, planned to move us out of this danger zone as soon as possible. Again a couple of huge tanks appeared with the feared Sikhs on top. Tall guns were aimed at the mountains while the guys quietly sat there eating their meals, all exposed to the sniper fire. We were in awe! About the same time lots of trucks drove up. This time they were

Allied army trucks. We were allowed to bring everything we wanted to take with us and we loaded it ourselves on the trucks. The sick from the hospital-house went first. In the meantime, the guns on the tanks occasionally fired a burst of warning shots up the mountains. Pure war! How could this be, we asked ourselves?

It was time for good-byes to our friends the Gurkhas. They seemed honestly sad to see us go. "Ships that pass in the night." This time we climbed on "friendly" trucks and were off. Where to now? Another camp and we were free . . . ?

Seventeen

Fort Willem I, Camp 9

FORT WILLEM I was named after a former Dutch ruler who at one time also was king of England. Fort Willem became a prison when forts were not needed anymore and the need for prisons arose. The truck ride was short and inside the fort we ended up in another very crowded room. It may have been a dining room as it was long and near the kitchens. The walls seemed about two meters thick. We had a corner on the outside wall and a window with heavy steel bars before it. We really felt like prisoners, although it also was a safe feeling. The fort was massive and solid, very large and easy to get lost in. We were free but we could not go anywhere. We were in prison. When was this going to end?

We did not know a soul in our room and there were hundreds of women and children in this camp. For safety's sake several Ambarawa camps had been assembled here as the attacks of the rebels had become a real threat. For the same reason we had been moved from Banjubiru. There were a few more men around who had come back from the war already to look for their families and wives. And the guards at the front entrance of the fort were British officers and soldiers with all their defense equipment. There were so many people here that they were even sleeping on the open galleries before the rooms.

After we arrived on the trucks with our barang, we quickly unloaded everything. The drivers asked for volunteers to go back to Banjubiru with a couple of trucks to get the rest of the *barang* and to get a few things that our other campmates had forgotten. I went with a couple of girlfriends.

Our Gurkhas came to greet us and many more soldiers had arrived on the premises. The two trucks were easily loaded. The Gurkhas invited us for tea and cookies, which we could not refuse. These were the friends who had visited us so often in our house near the gates. We did not stay long and then it was time for the real good-byes. Chris took me aside and politely asked me if I had time to sleep with him. I had not expected this at all and I explained to him that I could not do that but that he was still my friend. He smiled shyly and shook my hand. These brave little men showed real emotions and we felt that we truly had bonded with them in such a short time. When we left we waved until we could not see them any more.

Back in the fort, camp life continued in the same old way. Although the guards did not push us any more and the atmosphere was more relaxed, we felt that we wanted to move on now that we knew where Papa was.

We discovered that one of Papa's friends, a teacher at a college in Solo, was in our camp, a Mr. Bosman. He told us that at one time he had been in the same P.O.W. camp with Papa and he could tell us some stories. He said that Papa had arrived in Cilacap from Bandung after the Dutch army had capitulated and that he had been almost completely blind at that time. In the internment camp in Bandung the men had already been so severely starved that in Papa's case it had resulted in blindness.

Papa had unexpectedly met a doctor who had recognized him from Solo, but of course Papa could not see him. When they started talking the doctor had immediately taken him up into the hospital of the camp and had nourished him with several eggs a day and better meals. Luckily Papa's eyesight returned after a couple of weeks of improved hospital food. Papa's condition was the result of a severe shortage of proteins. We were all very pleased to hear that there had been a cure of simply better food. Mr. Bosman also told us that Papa later had been moved to a P.O.W. camp named Pakan Baru on the east side of Sumatra across from Singapore. He himself had stayed in Cilacap. When the war was over he had decided to move to Ambarawa as he had heard that there were so many women's camps, and he had thought that maybe he could help out. His own family was in Holland. He had taken on kitchen duties. He was a cheerful man and made us feel much better. We told him that Papa and Sietse were in Singapore and that eventually we were trying to get to that city.

By now we had heard that the war in Europe was also over. Here it was more than three months after our liberation on August 15 and we were still in the middle of all this misery. Actually, we were in another war zone. The shooting had become more serious. The fort was attacked by mortar fire at regular times. There were a lot of misses but the sound of the exploding shells was frightening. We just had to be on our guard.

With no forced labor anymore we had time to visit

other campmates and listen to some terrifying camp stories from the different camps around Ambarawa. For example, we heard that shortly before we had arrived at the fort, Camp Ambarawa 8 had been taken over by the *merdeka* men and they had ordered all the women and children up to the field near the front gates. From that point the rebels had thrown hand grenades into the crowd. In panic everyone had started to run away, but a few alert women had picked up some unexploded grenades and had thrown them right back at the extremists. It had been a mess! Fourteen people died and there were quite a few wounded. The British troops had driven the rebels out in a hurry, but the grief was acute for the families involved after such a tragedy. It was so sad to lose loved ones after all the miserable years under the Japanese, besides the suffering of renewed fear and anguish.

Our friend Bertha Harwig and her two little children had been in that camp. She had refused to obey the order. Instead, she had hidden herself and the kids under her bunk bed and, in doing so, had escaped the ordeal. She had counted hours, which actually had been only minutes, until it was all over. But her fear had been immense.

In another camp, during one of the last days before the war had ended, the women and children were also summoned up to the front of the camp. When they were all waiting on the little plaza, the Japs had started to beat into the crowds with rifle butts and sticks. In panic everyone had run to the opposite side of the field trying to escape, when from that end a group of Japs appeared to do the same thing. Women and children were falling and stumbling over each other while running back and forth. It had been a cruel scene and several persons were terribly hurt.

Luckily we were free from such horror, except that now

the mortar shells were falling into this fort. Still, life went on, breakfast, lunch, and dinner. We were getting some of our strength back.

Every night at ten o'clock the British at the front entrance sent up a thunderous warning signal by shooting all of the heavy artillery in several directions. We were told that they did this to inform the extremists that they were on guard. However, the *merdeka* men became much more thorough in their aiming and occasionally some mortar shells burst in the middle of the fort.

Early one morning when Ann was taking our night potty to the washrooms, a shell exploded right before our room. Ids had run out just ahead of her. Ann was hit in her shoulder by shrapnel and fell to the ground. We heard the "bang" and dropped to the floor inside our room.

People came running, "Mrs. Talsma, Mrs. Talsma, your daughter is hurt, your daughter is hurt!" At the same time Ids came running back to tell us. He did not even realize that his legs were cut up by small pieces of shrapnel from the shell. Mama ran out. Ann was lying on the ground and the people in the area were consoling her already. There was a lot of blood of course. Nurses came up with a stretcher and carried Ann to the little hospital, where she received the best of care. It was quite a commotion, we were in shock.

When Mama came back she could tell us that Ann was all right, no serious damage was done. She had to stay in hospital though, in case of complications. What a scare, what an anxiety, but we were relieved that she was not killed! More shells had fallen and there were more injuries. Ann told us later that it felt as if her whole shoulder had been shot off. She was lucky though, the shell part ricocheted off her shoulder blade and ribs, and came out on the side of her chest near her armpit.

The experts at the front entrance studied the angles and depths of the attacks and they figured out where the shells were coming from. Several *merdeka* guns were silenced by the return fire from our front artillery. It was a scary thing. From then on the organization of the fort started with the evacuation of the camp population, beginning with the sick and wounded and their families.

It was only a few days after this event that we saw ourselves climbing on a truck again with our few earthly possessions. We finally decided to leave our dirty mattresses behind. By now we were glad to get out of the mountains. We had been closed in long enough. Our first goal was Semarang. Mama had given Singapore as our destination and it felt good to say, "We are going to Singapore."

But we were not there yet. It was quite a convoy, military police included. The roads the trucks had to travel on were not there, they were all blown up by land mines. It turned out to be a very rough ride. We bumped and shook all the way. Several times we had to stop to avoid obstructions, deep craters, holes, and rocks on the road. The armed British soldiers who accompanied us removed or straightened as much of the debris as they could, otherwise it would not be possible to continue. Normally it is not too long a stretch from Ambarawa to Semarang, but now it was long enough for our skinny bodies to be shaken apart. We were not confronted by any rebels, which was a relief!

In Semarang they took us to an outlying villa area. Our truck stopped at a house which we could use all for ourselves. It was scarcely furnished but that did not bother us. Ann had to go to a hospital, we did not know where. The officer reassured us that she would be in good hands and safe. They promised that when we would move on, they would contact us and bring Ann along. Ann was pretty sore from the ride, especially with her wounded back. She must have felt quite lonely and frightened going to another strange hospital.

The whole area where we were was safe from rebels. Regular surveillance was run by British M.P.s and a check on the houses was included. We felt safe but restless. One reason for that was, that we were on our own as a family. It was so strangely quiet without all the other camp people around. But we were on the move. We had a destination and this was not it! The waiting was difficult. Who would come for us?

Eighteen

From Semarang to Batavia, Camps 10 and 11

I THINK THIS area was called Tjandi, but I am not sure as I did not know Semarang at all. Once I had been to this city with Papa to buy a baby carriage when little Pete was on the way. Papa and I went by train to shop in downtown Semarang since the choice of such an item was much bigger in that city. That had been quite an occasion for me. At any rate, I had not been on this hilly side of Semarang and in normal times it must have been a very desirable place to live. The villas were set on large properties and the winding streets around them were constructed in a very scenic way.

Our present house was roomy and we would have enjoyed it more if we had not been so anxious to move on. Also the fact that Ann was not with us worried us all. It was so nice that the little ones could play safely outside though. They had some of their strength back but were still so small and pale for a seven- and five-year-old. We older girls felt better too. Youth restores itself so quickly. Only three to four weeks after some more nourishing food, we all had our periods back already, which was very inconvenient on this trip. In a hurry we had cut up some old towels and cloths and had hand-sewn the necessary pads. Soap was back too but not the convenience of soaking, washing, and drying which was such an important part of this monthly process. In this humid heat of November nothing would dry. We had to take advantage of being in this big house and chores had to be done, including laundry. The most necessary clothes had to be washed.

Not even two days later a couple of trucks drove up. The officers who had dropped us off had told us to be ready to go in an instant when they came back for us. So, every morning we had packed up our things and put them near the front door. We were ready. Ann was already in the truck, smiling away. She felt much better and told us she had been treated well at the hospital. We loaded our backpacks and the rest of our *barang* and climbed on the truck ourselves.

Away we went! Boy, at high speed, with squealing wheels, we sped down the hilly streets and then the roads became rougher and straighter. They had told us we were going by air to Batavia and soon we saw it, the airport! We could see the outstretched fields and runways. Our truck headed for a transport plane that was sitting in the distance on the tarmac.

Suddenly, our truck made an about-face and we turned back onto the road. "What is happening?" we asked each other. But we did not get an answer until we had raced back down the same route and returned to the same house we had left such a short while ago. When stopped, the driver jumped out and explained. "I'm sorry," he said, "the airport was under heavy attack by the extremists and it would have been too risky to let any plane take off. We'll try again when it is safe. Just be ready again." And then they left. Ann stayed in the truck with them. She had to return to the hospital, by order of the officer in charge. But at least we had seen her and knew that she was alright.

Of course, we were disappointed, but we understood the danger and did not complain. We had experienced so many disappointments, this one was one with a promise—try again tomorrow!

Sure enough, the next morning the truck appeared again. The same British officers picked us up. Ann was with them. "We are going to try again," they smiled, "it seems quieter this morning." We went through the same fast ride down the hills and streets. The same airplane was sitting on the runway. When we approached it we noticed more women and children arriving. As soon as we climbed out of the truck we wanted to enter the plane, but it was so terribly hot inside that we hesitated. Some crew members advised us to wait a few moments outside till departure time. But when it was time to enter, the heat was suffocating. Around midday it normally is like an oven in an open space in the tropics, but inside the plane it seemed like the oven had been stoked up. There was no insulation inside and the body of the transport plane was one steel hulk with a ridge on the sides, but no seats at all. We had to sit on this hotplate or stand up. The little ones did not have shoes at all and they were tripping around on their bare feet trying to step on something like a mat or cloth to prevent their feet from frying. There was nothing. We gave them an old piece of matting to stand on. In minutes perspiration ran down our bodies, dripping down our faces, necks, and backs. The only air came through some open holes on the side of the hulk and everybody tried to get a hold of one to sniff up some cooler air. It was useless, the outside air was almost as hot. More and more people came in and went through the same panicky feelings of "no air." Luckily we had some wet cloths with us to wipe off the sweat, but it seemed like an eternity before the engines started and we moved. It was amazing how few people complained. We all wanted out of there and we all braved this live roast. Even the children were quiet. We sat on our backpacks until we were on the way, still wondering if there had been another attack on the airport.

This was our first airplane flight and it was wonderful. We were flying, and it seemed that I was dreaming. Maybe it was the heat and the smell of the sweat that made me feel queasy, but we were getting away. I had a feeling of elation when finally we climbed towards the clouds. Were we really free? I felt a deep thankfulness come over me. From now on it should become better.

It became cooler too and that relaxed the travelers. We started to look out of the side holes which served as ventilation and windows. We were flying over the Java sea and had a clear view of the coastline of our island Java. No one appeared nervous. One of the crew members apologized for the long wait. Apparently there *had* been another attempt to attack the airfield. To me it did not matter any more. We were flying away.

The little ones were also much happier and Peter glowed when he was allowed, in turn with other little boys, to come to the cockpit to see all the instruments and talk to the pilot. He came back all excited.

The flight lasted a good hour and a half and did not seem long at all. After landing however, the same thing happened. It was not because we were loaded onto trucks again, but the fact that the race was on from the airport Kemajoran to Camp Adek 2. We learned that it was just as treacherous driving through the city here in Batavia as it had been in Semarang. There were snipers everywhere and here also, the *merdeka* people had grabbed all the Japanese weapons and were trying to take over the country. The British, who had been put in charge of Southeast Asia by the Allied forces, had come six weeks too late. Besides, they had not allowed the Dutch volunteers to move on to the main islands. That was quite a revelation for us. Had they come sooner, then the extremists would not have had time to plan and attack the women's camps and many lives would have been saved!

Camp Adek 2, where we were taken, appeared to be a transit camp. Lots and lots of women and children were waiting for transport to their loved ones and family. Or they were just simply waiting for a husband and/or father to show up. We definitely saw many more men around.

Ann had to go back to another hospital. She was still not officially released. This time we inquired which hospital it was so that if we moved on, we could get in contact with her. Mama still worried a lot about it. She wanted us all together. Except for Ids, we had never been separated through all these years. We had made it so far and thanks to the Lord were in order. That night we slept on mattresses, all in a row, and dreamed about a future which now seemed possible.

Nineteen

The *Queen Emma*

AFTER A good night's sleep and some breakfast, Mama stepped up to the main office of Camp Adek 2. She asked if there were transportation available in the near future to Singapore where Papa would be waiting for us. She had taken the letter from Papa with her which we had received in Banjubiru. But there was no proof needed. "No problem," they said, "tomorrow a boat is heading out that way, you can be on it!" Mama came back all excited. "One more day", she said, "and then we are going to see Papa again."

The day went by, during which we tried to relax. We met several campmates from Sumowono and Ambarawa. Ids actually found a friend from Solo and from the boys' camp. This boy had been reunited with his mother and she was good friend of Mama. They were waiting in Adek for his father, her husband, to join them. Mrs. Van Goudoever also was a mother who had stayed behind alone in camp when her only son Jake was taken away. It had driven her almost over the brink to madness. She appeared fine and calm now. She and Mama had a good visit and, close as we were as a family, it did Mama good to talk with a friend.

Early the next day we received the message, "Be ready before noon, it is *go* today, by ship to Singapore!" We became all action. Our few belongings were already packed, but Ann still had to be picked up from the hospital somewhere in Batavia. Someone from the office had made contact with that hospital and it turned out that I was going to pick her up.

I waited at the front entrance of the camp for a car with a driver. Soon I was approached by an Ambonese man who spoke perfect Dutch. He told me that he was assigned to pick up Ann. He showed me some identification and after Mama and Emmy saw me off, we sped out of the campyard as if the devil was on our heels.

The man grinned and explained the reason for his haste. "We're now driving through the most dangerous part of Batavia," he said. "Here is where all the guerrilla fighting went on, but it is reduced to only snipers now. Still, the faster we move, the better our chances are of getting through unharmed." I told him that I was used to fast rides the last couple of days and explained how we had escaped out of Semarang.

I remember that I was not frightened at all. This man had such confidence and since he was a volunteer I thought he was pretty brave too, and I told him so. He acknowledged it gracefully and said, "It's the least I can do. You women and children suffered so much. I want to help." I told him in short what had happened to Ann, he looked grim and commented, "It should not have happened, it just shouldn't!"

It was quite a distance but because of our speed, we reached the emergency hospital in no time. Some of our own soldiers stood on guard at the entrance. The driver showed his identification and we moved in. He drove right to the barrack where Ann was supposed to be. And yes, she was dressed and ready to go. We girls exchanged the latest news about our trip to Singapore while we were racing back through the same district.

The trucks were waiting for us when we arrived. We thanked our chauffeur and said good-bye. He wished us a good trip and a good life. Mama and the others were ready. Mama had all her chickens back with her and that alone made her day. We were all so happy that Ann had recovered so well without complications. In our undernourished and weakened condition, infections were very common, but luckily her wounds were healed. Only her shoulder was still somewhat stiff. At the hospital the food had been perfect, which also added to her recovery.

There wasn't much time to reminisce. The trucks were waiting to take us to the harbor Tandjong Priok. Ann and I just transferred from the car to the truck and when the truck was full, once more we were driven at high speed to our destination, the harbor.

The ship was waiting. Now we were leaving our country. As soon as we set foot on the minesweeper, the *Queen Emma*, we left our beloved country behind. At that time we did not realize it. So much had happened the last few weeks and this was another step for our safety. The beautiful island we were about to vacate would be buried deep in our hearts. It was where we grew up, where we thrived, where we were happy. God had saved us all for some reason and we were so grateful, but we had to move on.

The *Queen Emma* was a perky little ship. Even if it was a minesweeper it had to be used to transfer P.O.W.'s and women and children. There was a shortage of transportation ships and every available boat was thrown in for this purpose. Everything was so clean, the scrubbed decks, the nice little cabins, good food in a cozy dining room. It was not too crowded although the ship was full with women and children. For safety's sake the ship took off in the late afternoon but overnight it stayed just outside the harbor. There had been some skirmishes with the rebels at the harbor and we would leave early the next morning.

After a good meal Mama took Peter and Elly to one of our little cabins where they soon drifted off in their bunk beds. That first night we all went to sleep rather early because it had been such an exciting day.

We took off early the next morning. It was a beautiful day, but Mama had to spend part of it with Peter at the ship's doctor's clinic. The last couple of days Peter had developed a swelling on his elbow. A lot of people were running around with such infectious camp sores, which were a result of all the dirt we had been eating in the camps. The doctor had to drain the sore and Peter was so brave. Small as he was, he had learned to endure more than a normal child his age. His pain was soon forgotten when he held a chocolate bar in his little hands which the doctor gave him. He had never seen or tasted such a delicacy in his life. We were pretty proud of him.

That evening after dinner Emmy and I explored the ship's decks. We met some cheerful sailors who were off duty and we practiced our English. It was late when they escorted us to our cabins. Very satisfied, we slept more peacefully than we had done in ages while the ship steamed on to Singapore.

After two days, we arrived in Singapore. What a busy harbor! Several ships were docked there with people from the Japanese concentration camps onboard. The *Queen Emma* wormed herself alongside the quay also. As she was a low ship we had a good view of the hustle and bustle ashore. We scanned the crowds for familiar faces but there were none, no Papa either. We saw soldiers, sailors, British as well as Dutch, and other nationalities. There were navy men, airmen, civilians, dock workers of all nations and every single one seemed to be in a hurry.

The Red Cross people came onboard our ship to see if there were any sick people who needed hospitalization. These were taken ashore first with their families. We did not report Ann. We had seen her scars and she was completely healed. Then a welcoming committee arrived and we were all invited to come along so that we could get directions to a temporary camp. We had no money at all, so we were taken with another truck to the Irene Camp, approximately twenty-five kilometers outside Singapore. We learned that most camps with Dutch women and children were named after the Dutch royal family and there were quite a few.

In a way it was a let-down, but our spirits were high. We really had hoped that Papa would have been there on the quay. Mama had mailed him a postcard saying that we were on the way! So especially for Mama it must have been a disappointment, but then, weren't we used to disappointments? At last, we were free, finally—free from attacks, unexpected shelling, snipers and hurts.

We found an empty little side room on the second floor of a huge building block. We were provided with mattresses and had to sleep flat on the floor again. It did not bother us. Everything was different again, particularly the presence of men around was impressive. We were not used to men any more. But where was Papa? There was no way we could contact him, but tomorrow was another day.

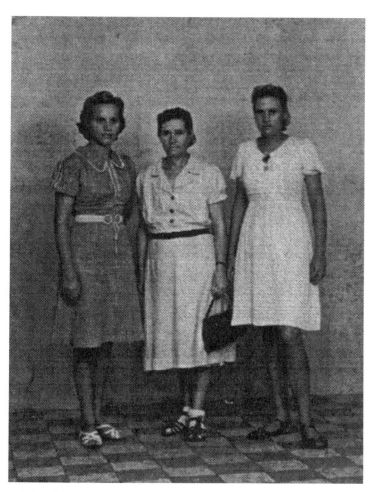

Joke, Mama, and Emmy in Singapore, 1946.

Papa in Singapore, December 1945.

My family in Holland, including brother Sietse *(standing, second from left)*, summer 1946.

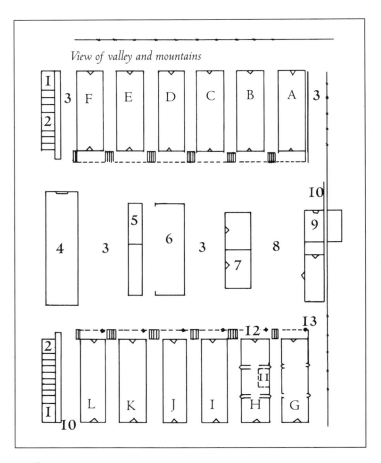

Sumowono, camp 5

1 - bathrooms
2 - toilets
3 - roadway
4 - horse stables
5 - firewood & storage
6 - kitchens

7 - storerooms
8 - assembly field
9 - guardhouse
10 - gate
11 - our living area
12 - open gallery with steps
leading down to paved road

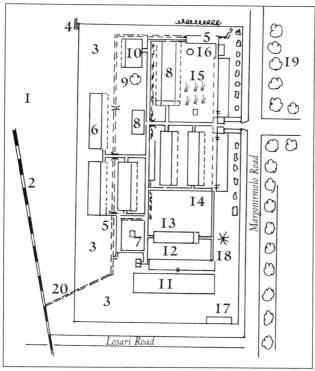

Ambarawa, camp 6

1 - Sawah's rice fields
2 - railroad tracks
3 - gardens
4 - watch post (from time when Ambarawa was an NSB* camp)
5 - bath and latrines
6 - empers (covered galleries)
7 - death house (morgue)
8 - boys' barracks
9 - djambu tree
10 - kitchen

11 - assembly field on tennis courts
12 - barracks for the sick and dying
13 - medical clinic
14 - little lawn
15 - washlines
16 - well
17 - stable
18 - kernei palm
19 - fairgrounds
20 - latrine ditch

*This former military hospital was first a camp in which members of the NSB (Nationale Socialistische Bond) were interned by the Dutch government between 1940 and 1942, and then a Japanese prison camp from 1942–1945. From December 23, 1942 to March 26, 1944 the camp was under civil command. From March 26, 1944 to August 24, 1945 the camp was under Japanese military command. Between 1942 and 1945, 1,150 women and children were sent to Ambarawa from Kedu, Wonosobo, Sumowono, and Cihapti. From January 3–5, 1945 the women and children were moved to Solo and Muntilan, and 1,200 sick old men from Cimahi arrived at Ambarawa. Boys eleven years and older stayed behind in this camp which from then on was called "Deathcamp" as 90 percent of the men from Cimahi died there.

    This map was adapted from one drawn by Bert Philippens, who was interned in this camp from December 23, 1942 to August 26, 1945.

Gate and guardhouse entrance, Muntilan, camp 7

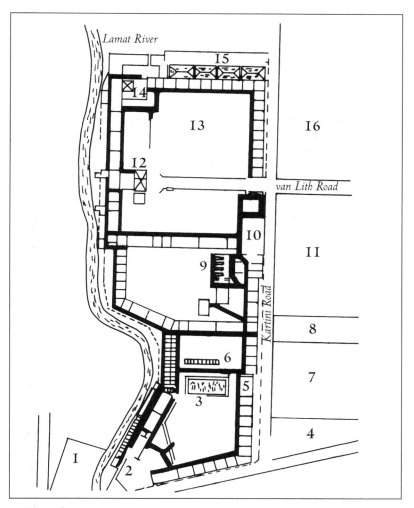

Muntilan, camp 7

1 - Javanese cemetery
2 - recreation room (women/children)
3 - dirty swimming pool
4 - cemetery
5 - our room
6 - latrines over ditch
covered with bamboo
7 - monastery
8 - school

9 - kitchen
10 - church
11 - open (sports) field
12 - main building
13 - assembly field
14 - camp hospital
15 - heiho buildings
16 - kampong

Inside entrance, Muntilan

Main building,
Muntilan

Twenty

Singapore I, Camp Irene, Number 12

WE AGAIN woke up in strange surroundings. My first thoughts were, "We are free! We are really free!" I got up as soon as the sun showed its face and so did everybody else. We were so excited. We chatted about the fact that we were here in Singapore, away from the Japs and the other attackers, like the *merdeka* fighters.

We wondered how this world can be so full of hatred that a man can shoot at helpless women and children. And that one country can hate another country so much that it seems normal to torture and starve innocent civilians. We talked about the Indies we left behind, our land, our youth, Papa's life's work. Then Mama said, "But Holland is also beautiful. We'll go back there and you'll see, it is very beautiful. But we will have to wait till Papa comes back first. I hope it won't be long until he finds us."

We agreed and we were happy already. I said that I was going to do the laundry. We had practically nothing to wear any more but the clothes on our backs and they were dirty too. During the last weeks there hardly had been a chance to wash a thing. A family of eight accumulates quite a bit of laundry even if it is all worn out.

In the meantime, someone from the organization committee of this camp came by with information about meals and also with instructions regarding rules and regulations. Then we could pick up bread and butter and jam and meats. We had a real breakfast together. Bread . . . out of this world! We had not seen real bread for years, at least not like this.

It was already around 9:00 A.M. when I finally started my wash. Ids and I had carried a couple of pails of water from the washrooms up onto the verandah which bordered on the side of the colossal center room. I had my hands full of suds when Ids raced by me and disappeared in our little side room. At about the same moment I heard a man's voice behind me say in Dutch, *"Hallo Joke, hoe gaat het?"* ("Hello Joke, how are you?") I turned around and looked up.

"Sietse!" I exclaimed. "How did you get here?"

Here stood my brother Sietse from Holland. We hugged and kissed. Emmy, Ann, Lies, and the little ones came running out of the side room to see what all the commotion was about. They were getting their turn in the greetings.

But then, Papa walked up on the verandah. We shrieked and hugged and smiled. Papa just cried. Mama was still inside the little room. Now, I don't know who it was, but one of us guided Papa to Mama and then we left them alone. I did not see their reunion, I felt it was their private moment!

Meanwhile, Sietse examined all his five sisters and two brothers whom he had not seen for over six years. He had never even met his baby sister Elly, who was now five years old. They became good friends right away. And we all were admiring him. He was in an air force uniform, almost six feet six inches tall, handsome as Adonis and we were completely stunned. Not only about our long lost brother, but also about the fact that he was here!

Then we went into the side room to see and greet Papa who was sitting with Mama on the half made-up mattresses. They were in each others arms. Mama had been straightening up the beds when Ids had raced in to tell her that Papa was on the way. Even if she was prepared, she was still somewhat in shock when Papa walked in moments later. He was so thin and pale. He cried when he greeted every single one of his children. He could not speak at all. The emotion was heavy and we young people felt we should change the mood slightly by pushing Sietse into the room.

I'll never forget Mama's face! "Oh, my boy, oh Sietse, you are here too. How is this possible?" They hugged and kissed each other. This tall young man bending over his small thin mother, it was a miracle!

Small and thin as she was, she was not shy. "We must have some good food ordered in, whatever," she said. "We have to have lunch together." The men had money. Now our whole family, Papa, Mama and all eight children had lunch. We thanked the Lord from the bottom of our hearts that we could be together again, that we had been spared while so many others had lost their lives.

Of course, one story after another came up and the questions and answers never stopped. Sietse told us how he and Papa had found us. A lady from our ship, the *Queen Emma*, whose husband was in the same camp as Papa, had told Papa that we had been onboard. But at the time he heard the good news we had left for Camp Irene already.

Nobody knew that. Papa had picked up Sietse from his camp. The officer in charge had given him permission to stay out in order to find his family.

Then Papa and Sietse had taken a cab and had gone from camp to camp to inquire at the head offices if a large family had arrived that day. But the result was very disappointing, we were not registered anywhere. Unless it would be the last camp Irene, twenty-five kilometers out of town, near the village of Nee Soon. The cab driver got lost, so they ended up back at the Wilhelmina camp, the center point of all camps in downtown Singapore.

It was fate, or luck, or whatever, that they ran into an old friend of Papa from Solo who was still in military service and stationed in Nee Soon. When Papa explained what he and Sietse had been doing all night (it was close to midnight by then), the man said that they could have a ride with him in his truck. They had quickly arrived at the Irene camp while talking away about old times.

The man waited while Papa and Sietse went inside the building to inquire at the office if we had arrived. And yes, it was confirmed. Then they went into the big rooms with a flashlight trying to discover a large sleeping family, without luck. They did not know of course, that we had been in the little side room. Anyhow, they were grateful that their friend had waited as it had become too late and they decided to continue their search the next morning. They found a place to sleep and as Papa was so terribly tired, it had actually been a blessing in disguise that they could not find us.

This same morning when they were walking on the big plaza around the camp they had recognized Ids going to the kitchen to get hot water for tea. With Sietse calling and

Papa whistling our well known family whistle, Ids, somewhat confused, had come up to them to greet them. Then Ids had guided them quickly to our second-floor room.

Papa turned out to be a very sick and tired man. The Japanese had done a good job on him! He was full of sores and boils all over his body, he had hunger edema, pellagra, and malaria. He was under regular doctor's care.

Papa had been in Singapore for a couple of weeks after returning from camp Pakan Baru on West Sumatra, when he heard that a lot of young airmen had arrived from Holland who were sitting in a camp near the ocean just outside Singapore. As Papa knew that Sietse always wanted to become a flyer, he had an intuition that Sietse could be among them. So, Papa had taken a cab and, with an old friend, they had found the camp. The red-cheeked guard at the entrance confirmed Papa's question. "Yes, Talsma was there!"

Papa received instructions about where to go and soon he ran right into the son he had not seen for so long. He stopped a couple of young airmen on a path between the tents and said, "Hello Sietse, my boy."

Sietse had looked up inquisitively. He did not recognize his father! It was a big shock to him to discover the state his father was in when he realized that it *was* Papa. Papa looked so awfully sick, Sietse had no idea this was the same father he had left six years ago in Solo. From then on they spent a lot of time together, scanning lists of incoming ships from Java to find out if we were on them.

Holland had been liberated in May, 1945, and now it was early December, 1945. There had been a lot of changes in Holland, but Sietse had been adamant to leave and find his family in the Indies, not knowing if anyone would still be alive. He had joined the air force immediately after the war in Europe was over, with the purpose of getting away. On arrival in Singapore the British had very diplomatically and politically refused to send these troops to the main islands of the Netherlands East Indies. The result had been that the liberation of the P.O.W. camps was delayed until after the 15th of August 1945. "Why?" we asked. Had there not been enough suffering?

But Sietse had made himself useful by searching the survivors lists of P.O.W. camps in the hope of finding his father's name. Papa had found him instead! It had been an unexpected and unbelievable reunion! Papa still had regular malaria attacks and had to rest a good part of his days, that's why Sietse had visited Papa more often.

But now we were all together. We felt so happy. It was just as if we had received a big present and, actually, we had. Papa had to go for a rest after all the emotions. He had not slept much the night before and his poor body was worn out. Luckily we had that little side room so that he could have a quiet nap. Later on he went to the head office to make arrangements with his camp and ours to transfer to our camp, as he wanted to stay with us, of course. Sietse could stay one night, then he had to join his troop again.

His camp was set in Changi on the opposite side of Singapore and the Irene camp, quite far from us. "But I'll be back," he said with wink and a smile, "and I'll bring some boyfriends along for you girls!" We wholeheartedly agreed that we, by now, should be in for some exciting changes in our daily routines.

Twenty-One

Singapore II, Camp Irene

SURE ENOUGH, Singapore was wild. Wild with happy, liberated, but also a lot of very sick, people. The city was full. Talk about overpopulation! The camps were crowded with all the Dutch ex-prisoners of war. Besides these camps, there were the British, Australian, and American military camps, which also included volunteer troops from Europe who had come to help liberate the Far East. There were army, navy and air force men in all shapes, sizes, and color. Then of course, there was the original population. From early in the morning till late at night the streets were filled with life, busy life. The city never slept. Army trucks and jeeps and all other kinds of military vehicles were king of the road. This was freedom, I felt so relaxed.

In the meantime, we had been asked to vacate our little side room, which we all regretted. The camp organizers needed this room for administration purposes and first aid and that made sense. But it had been such a nice quiet place for Papa to rest, particularly when his malaria attacks occurred. We moved just around the corner from it into the large main room. We put up curtains in the form of *tikers* and old drapes. I don't know where they came from. It gave us a bit more privacy, just as in Sumowono. Getting used to the noise again was no problem, that was still ingrained in our heads as normal. We had mattresses on the floor. During the day we lived mostly on the open verandah, except when it rained.

Most camp people had all kinds of infections, from pus-filled camp sores and boils to the so-called monkey-pox. These last ones looked like chicken pox but they popped up on the most atrocious warm places of our bodies. Under our arms, between legs and in any creases. They were very itchy and contagious, but harmless. The clinic treated them with a strong disinfectant. Then they dried up. We were told that it was a result of eating all that junk in the prison camps. It had to take its time to clear out of our blood, said the doctors. Everybody had them. It was a nuisance, as every day we stood in line at the clinic to get treated. "Eat a lot of fruit and vegetables," was the advice and we tried to. The central kitchen provided perfect food and plenty of it. More and more people were able to buy additional provisions. So did we, mostly fruits. Although we could not cook for ourselves, we could get enough hot water for coffee and tea. Sietse and his friends often treated us with treats like cakes or cookies.

By the middle of December we had met quite a few interesting young men, also some British officers and navy men. They came to visit the camps to look for company and seemed to enjoy family life; primitively as we lived, they did not seem to mind. They liked the Dutch girls and were very sympathetic about our past experiences and thought it was dreadful that we were made to live here in this camp as we did!

Christmas was coming up and as a family we could not do much, specifically because Papa was still too weak to endure the activities required for a party. That's why we were so thrilled when the British navy officers invited us to a Christmas dinner and dance on board their cruiser. Emmy, Ann, and I accepted with pleasure and Papa and Mama were happy for us. We had not celebrated anything for years, Christmas included. The officers would pick us up and they promised us a most wonderful evening.

However, around the 20th of December, I developed a huge boil on my thigh. I could not even walk and I was so sore. Like everyone else I had suffered through the monkey-pox and I was almost clear of it and now this! Boils were terrible. I wanted to go to this Christmas dinner so badly. All day long, day after day I soaked this ugly thing with whatever would brew it open. As luck would have it, on the morning of Christmas day it broke and drained. I still had to rest my leg a lot but I could walk and go to the party!

We put on our best available dresses and when the truck came to pick us up, we were driven to the harbor where the huge British cruiser was docked. We saw many more of our friends there and also families with children. There were beautifully decorated tables in the festive dining rooms and we were served hand and foot by all these smiling young sailors. A delicious turkey dinner with all the trimmings and plum pudding for dessert. It was such a treat!

Afterwards Fred, my date, sat down with me on the deck because I was still bandaged up and could not dance, but he did not mind. He was such a gentleman. Emmy danced with Johnny, a jovial sailor who was also one of our escorts. They seemed to have a good time.

I enjoyed myself immensely despite sitting all night. The little colorful lights, the view of Singapore harbor, the huge ship, the happy people on it, it all added to my feeling of freedom. It surely wiped out a lot of my sad experiences of only a month ago.

The trucks for Camp Irene left by midnight. Fred and Johnny rode back with us. Johnny had had a little bit too much to drink but he was very funny. As soon as we arrived back in our room, we found a spot for him and Fred to sleep on a corner of a mattress near the boys. It was holiday time and they were off the next day. They proved to be such good friends and we had enjoyed such a wonderful evening.

In the morning we boasted of course about our turkey dinner, but apparently the family had celebrated also and had eaten a special meal prepared in the kitchens. We were glad. Fred and Johnny left in the afternoon. Occasionally they came back to see us. They always brought something along, such as treats and little gifts for Peter and Elly. Soon after New Year their cruiser left Singapore and we never heard from them again.

Sietse mostly came on weekends and he also brought the promised friends along. Everyone tried to please us so much, it was such a good feeling. We had been so abused the past four years that we drank in any kindness as a healing medicine. One of Sietse's friends, Kees, became quite a good friend of mine but just for the time in Singapore. We were honestly attracted to each other. It was good to talk and spend time with a young man.

On New Year's Eve the boys in Changi camp threw a party to which we also were invited. They did not serve dinner but everyone individually had friends and girlfriends over for a barbecue or meal on the lawns. They had strung up little lights and lampions all over the place, it looked so romantic and festive. We had a ride to the Wilhelmina camp, the central point in Singapore. From there different trucks drove off in all kinds of directions to various destinations. Because so many people were strangers in the city these trucks were available as a goodwill to the camps.

The trucks for Changi were chockfull that night but we all arrived safely. The boys received us with open arms and this time I could dance. We had such an exciting evening. All together, we counted down the seconds into the new year. All these happy young people together made me think again, "How different was it just a month ago!" I was grateful, I was free but ... would I always compare the "now" and the "then?"

Even if the parties were fantastic, I was tired when I came home. When I woke up the next morning, I would still be in a camp sleeping on the floor. There was laundry to be done by hand in a little tub, water to be carried, sick family to attend to, while we were waiting for the time we could return to Holland. Sometimes the days seemed so wasted. But there were so many families in the same situation. Not only Dutch families, but also Dutch and British military men had to be repatriated. It took time to arrange for ships to be available. But it added to the time we had to spend in these circumstances.

For a change we went on a shopping spree in downtown Singapore. Mama had said so often, "The children need shoes, they have no shoes at all. They were babies when we went into the camps and I don't even know their sizes any more." To Mama the epitome of poverty was having no shoes. Thus, several of us, Papa, Mama, Peter and Elly, Liesje and I went by camp truck to a downtown truck stop from where we walked by all the shops, boutiques, and stores to find shoes for the kids.

Boy, was it busy down those streets! The merchants were

running out of their little shops to invite the customers in. They wanted to sell so badly, they praised their wares in several languages. We found shoes for the children and Mama was happy. It was so much fun but Papa tired very rapidly. It was very hot. Singapore's temperature predominantly lingers around the 31°–32° Celcius mark. We decided to return to camp. But it had been good for us all to be out.

We had such outings more often when a friend of Papa from Solo showed up one day. He told me he had been thinking about me a lot while in the Japanese camps and he wondered if we could have a relationship. I kindly let him know that I was sorry but that I did not have any feelings for him. I really could not make out if he was disappointed. If he was like all other P.O.W.s he probably could hide a disappointment very well; there had been so many in our lives! He offered to take us shopping once or twice, which was fun. We did not have any money and we could not accept gifts all the time but I have good memories of these trips. Just to do what we wanted to do. It was a healing time, a time to get better. We did gain strength by the day due to good food and less stress.

Papa was in the worst condition. He was often quiet and he cried about anything and nothing. That was not our Papa. He always used to be strong and knew what to do. In all my years I had never seen Papa cry so often, but we understood that he had been close to death. He remained under doctor's care as long as we were in Singapore. Our edemas had practically disappeared by now, although when I had been out on very hot humid days, my feet and ankles would swell up again in no time. It was a slow process. So many years of hunger could not be wiped out in a couple of weeks. We were told that after two years symptoms could still pop up, and they did.

Some families experienced very sad things. Quite a few women had become completely independent through the war years. They were used to making decisions for their children and about other important matters which had come up in family life, but now that the husbands were back it appeared that they could not talk things over any more. It happened that several couples split up because of this difficulty. Most of the children had a hard time believing that this was possible and so did we.

The weeks crept by and it could be pretty hot up on our floor. In another camp there was an outbreak of polio and we were advised to rest more and take it easy. But some days Emmy and I hitchhiked to Changi to visit Sietse and our new friends. Everyone was always so friendly. During those days we were never attacked or insulted. My memories of Singapore are good. We lived there slightly over two months.

Rumor had it that more ships were available for repatriating P.O.W.s but we never received notice. On the first day of February 1946 Emmy told us that a couple of girlfriends were leaving for Holland and we were hopeful that our turn might come also. As quite a few families had left our room already it became quieter, but it also made us more anxious. When was it going to be our turn? Then Liesje stormed into the room on the morning of the fourth of February. She was so excited, "The man in the office told me that we are on the list, it's true, it's true!"

Papa confirmed the message and from then on it went fast. We had to be ready on the fifth of February to board the *Alcantara*, a British troop transport ship. Sietse had come to Singapore on it when he left England. Papa and Mama went into Singapore to pick up some necessary items which we could use in Holland, while we cleaned up and packed as well as we could. We were told that the ship could hold three thousand men. How would this work out? But never mind, we were going. It was also time to say good-bye to all our newly-made friends. One way or other we informed Sietse and Kees of our news. Would this be the last of so many moves?

Twenty-Two

Ids' And Papa's Stories

AT THE END of September, 1944, when Ids walked out of camp Ambarawa 2 with all the other boys, they soon arrived in Camp 8, the St. Louis school, also in Ambarawa. Most of the boys from the other camps were assembled there plus a lot of old men and a group of nuns. These last ones had the task of keeping the kitchens going and looking after the organization of the camp.

Ids became involved with camp chores right away, so did all the other boys. As soon as we left Camp 2 in early January 1945, the boys were moved to our former camp which was called Camp 7 from then on.

The nuns and men moved with them, while the group of old men that came out of the boarded-up train were transported to their camp also. The boys had also been at the train station late in the afternoon because the Japanese guard, Kano, or "Hansel my slave," had given several boys a chance to realize that their families were leaving Ambarawa. That's when we saw Ids under the little light bulb on the station's overhang.

Ids had been elected to one of the work groups as commandant over twenty boys and what they had to do was dig ditches, chop wood in the forests, work the fields, and carry bags of rice, sugar, corn, or flour out of railway depots to be distributed to all the camps around. Hard work for little boys of ten years old and up.

Of course the whole camp was starved slowly and when in the course of the year most of the old men started to die off one after another, Ids was promoted to one of the groups who had to help prepare for their burial. The group was called up by an announcement, "Work group Talsma, appear with shirts on!" This meant that they had to assemble at the death house where the dead were lying side by side on little *tikers*. The boys would call out "heads" or, "tails," and then they would lift up their load, mat and all, and tip it over into the coffin made of a heavier *gedek*. In the tropics a dead person has to be buried on the same day because the decomposing process starts immediately. So sometimes the decomposition fluids ran out of the bamboo coffins. The boys then had to carry the coffin to the gates and usually loaded it on a *grobak* (an oxen drawn cart). Nobody knows where these poor old men got their last resting place. Why the shirts? The Japanese commander said it was "to honor the dead!" On one day, Ids said, they carried seventeen dead men to the gates.

To think of it made Mama and Papa sick. The boys were sort of immune to the facts of death, it just happened too often. These boys, who should have been going to school getting an education, playing soccer and swimming, who should have eaten nourishing meals, being in their puberty, were abused, roughly handled as if they were tools, and left to stink in the dirt of a camp full of lice, fleas, cockroaches, and bedbugs.

Sometimes they did dishes or little private chores for the old men, who were completely weakened by starvation. The men would leave a tiny spoonfull of food on the plates to be washed and the more plates you had to wash the more extra bites to eat you would get. No wonder the infectious illnesses rampaged through the camp. The boys tried to find food in all kinds of ingenious ways. Some had to take care of the pigs destined for the guards' table. The animals lived generally on the kitchen scraps from the Japanese kitchens. But this food was still more nutritious than the camp food, thus the boys dealt with each other about the distribution of this pig food. The poor guys, some were so desperate that from the *slokan,* a latrine ditch that ran through the camp, they fished up undigested corn and native grown beans called *kedelee,* and after rinsing those off, they would eat them. Ids said that he had never been able to do that, but he had helped some friends to gather them.

The Japs were very rough and yelled a lot at the boys but Ids cannot remember that they were tortured, while this definitely did happen to the men. Some were cruelly beaten and punished for next to nothing.

It was just as if there was a specific plan to kill off as many old men as possible through starvation and mistreatment. It was not that there was no food available, as right after the defeat of Japan, truckloads of everything entered the camps everywhere. In this camp 90 percent of the old men perished.

When Ann and I picked Ids up he had been terribly sick and had just somewhat recovered. Luckily the war ended when it did, we had our brother back!

With Papa it was a similar process. From Bandung, the city where he was during the capitulation in 1942, he was put into a P.O.W. camp right away. Then Papa and the other men were just starved from the first days on. No food would come in, there was only water to drink until someone would remember, "Oh yes, these men eat too!" But then the provisions were so erratic that Papa became practically blind. With a large group of prisoners he was sent to Cilacap, a place on the south coast in central Java where he literally ran into doctor Pruys, the mission doctor he knew from Solo, who saved Papa's eyesight by caring for him in the right way. After the war we heard that Dr. Pruys was also shipped to Pakan Baru where, as a surgeon, he performed the most delicate operations in the most primitive circumstances with miraculous results.

When Papa, with a lot of other P.O.W. men, was transferred to Batavia waiting for transport to Sumatra, he was weak but not sick. At this time it was May, 1944. The day arrived when a coal ship was available and then the men were loaded in like sardines in a can. They were sitting with their knees pulled up under their chins or standing side by side in the hold of the ship. Hanging from ropes, boards were fastened to the upper decks. The men were sitting on these wobbly contraptions. There was one little drum as a latrine for all these thousands of men.

Their little bundles of luggage were dumped in the center of the hold and no one could move. For over two days they sat in the stinking, dysentery-infected coal bins. The sick were never able to reach the overflowing drum. Some men went stark crazy and were hard to calm down. No food was provided, just a sip of some brackish water now and then. There was one ladder to climb out of this hole and the stench in the heat of day and the cold of night were unbelievable. The men were black with sweat and coal dust mixed and the very sick men had to draw on their last resources in order to try and survive this ordeal. Several did not make it.

When they finally arrived in Padang harbor on the west coast in the center of Sumatra, the men were exhausted. As soon as they stepped ashore, though, a tropical rainstorm poured down on them, which was received as a blessing from above. The rain came down in buckets. The men had cheered and rubbed themselves clean of the coal dust and other dirt. They drank it, it cooled down their hot bodies and revived their courage. Maybe you'll have an idea by now what a tropical rain storm can do in this hot country, particularly for these men after what they had experienced in the dirty holds of the ship.

Papa did not tell much about his stay in camp Pakan Baru where he ended up. After a couple of days in Padang prison he was trucked through the most wonderful mountainous regions of Sumatra to the east coast. The Japanese had set up fourteen camps from the east to the west coast. With the help of thousands of Romushas, mostly Javanese slave laborers who were lured out of the *dessas* (villages) with false promises, the men had to lay a railroad through the thickest, swampiest jungle in the tropics. It was called "'The death railroad of Pakan Baru." Papa had to carry steel railroad beams on his shoulders all day long while the flooding rivers would wash out the basic dikes worked up by the Romushas.

Papa told us that once when a stretch of railway was completed, the Japanese had put a heavy locomotive on it to proudly show off that their plan was working. As soon as the engine started moving, the dike with the tracks on had promptly split and the big iron monster had nose-dived into the mud. The men who had worked on the line had burst out laughing, which drove the Japanese guards wild with fury. They started beating the prisoners closest to them but there were just too many to beat up and it was too hot. Thus the men were punished by letting them stand in the hot tropical sun for two days in a row. One after another had collapsed, but they were not allowed to be moved into the shade. No food, no drink was provided, only at night had they been able to go to their huts. Papa said he had endured it, but had suffered severe sunburn and dehydration. Such incidents were commonplace and a terror to think back on.

The railroad connection between east and west would improve the Japanese transports of goods but their main purpose was to be able to move weapons and ammunition from coast to coast. The increased show of Allied submarines on the west coast of Sumatra was intensely feared by the Japanese. Although the Allies did not realize it, they torpedoed a couple of ships full of P.O.W. men. The Japanese made the ships look like warships by placing artillery and canons on the decks. The Japanese captains had acted very nervous and mean, as they knew they could expect to be attacked at any time while moving the prisoners. Papa was lucky that it did not happen to his ship, however bad the trip was.

The men assembled in these camps lived in native huts with thatched roofs that leaked like baskets. When they stepped from their *bale-bales* (wooden boards), their bare feet would be covered with mud because of the rains and overflowing rivers. The jungle dampness brewed hordes of mosquitoes which resulted in malaria, dysentery, bugs, and moulds, killing the men like flies. The Romushas were completely left to fend for themselves and after long, cruel labored workdays they had to find their own food in the jungle. Sometimes the men could hear their cries for help in the distant jungle, "Tulung, tulung!" The Dutch and British prisoners were strictly forbidden to associate themselves with these poor men. They were threatened with thorough beatings or worse. Often the dead bodies of the slaves were found in the jungle, completely wasted. Within a year over twenty-three thousand men died in this hell hole, most of whom were Romushas.

The civilians, engineers, doctors, lawyers, plantation men, teachers like Papa, and military men were all doing slave labor under the most atrocious circumstances, to which none of them had ever been subjected in their lives. The Japs beat and abused and starved the men and enjoyed doing it. They seemed to hate tall men with blue eyes. Papa said he always kept his eyes down. If he looked them straight in the eye he could surely expect a slap in his face, which had happened on one occasion. Right after the soldier hit Papa, he had offered him a cigarette, which Papa could not refuse, of course. But Papa said he could have thrown it in the guy's face.

Several of the men had been able to bring money with them. They came from all over the archipelago and some had not been deprived of all their possessions. In this way, some men could buy food from the natives, even if it had to be smuggled in. It helped pass the time. Papa said that when he was in a "sick" camp he had sold hot coffee out of an old pail. This way he could gather up some money to buy an occasional extra meal. However, all this extra dealing was eventually forbidden and the men relied completely on the kitchens. As anywhere else, there was nothing to live on.

Papa was one of the first very seriously ill people to be moved out of the region to Singapore when this horrendous ordeal finally ended. After hearing these stories we realized how frightened and deserted Papa must have felt going through this misery alone.

Papa never became his old self again, though he never complained or lamented about the war years. After the war he tried four times to return to what was then called Indonesia to continue his career, but every time the doctors told him, "Give it up T., you are not fit enough for that country any more." People would say, "Tropical years count for two," which means, they take twice as much out of you as living in a cool climate. But Papa did it before the war and if he had not suffered so much in the prison camps he could have done it again.

Papa taught in the Dutch schools and he gave it his best. He was deeply hurt by the termination of his life's work. But we had a superb father back who also realized how much he had missed his whole family when they were growing up.

Twenty-Three

The *Alcantara I*

FINALLY, THE LONG wait was over. I was glad, it had been somewhat boring living in the slowly emptying camp the last couple of weeks. Now we had a purpose. We had slept another two months on the floor in this big room in Camp Irene, maybe it was time to get a bed. Now we were going to Holland. Would it mean a better life? Would we be able to continue our schooling? That had all been halted for a good four years. I was sixteen before the war, almost through high school, and now I was about twenty-one. Could I go back to school after five years? Still, I guessed I would have a better chance back in Holland than in the Indies.

On Java and the rest of the islands there was war, war for independence. Besides, Papa could not work anymore, if ever. He was a beaten man at almost forty-six. Luckily he had recovered somewhat during the last weeks, but he was always so tired. We wondered how many ruined lives had come out of this war.

Mama was on the mend also and although she still looked so small and pale, you had to admire her spunk and ambition for her family. These traits had helped her and us all through the terrible camp years.

And now, we were packed up. Still carrying our backpacks and a couple of new suitcases, we climbed on the truck that drove us to the harbor. Good-bye Camp Irene! Good-bye good memories. We had time to heal!

It was a madhouse on the quay. Hundreds of people ran around with their eyes looking up. The *Alcantara* was so high and huge, we had to drop our heads in our necks in order to see the top decks and bridge. At a checkpoint we were marked off a list, received some instructions and then climbed the long high gangway to enter another world.

Our first aim was to find sleeping places down in the quarters assigned for this purpose. The women and children were in mid-ship or center, where they could find a bunk or hammock. The men and bigger boys were in the front holds, but all that was easier said than done. The ship was full already when we arrived. We could never sleep together as a family. With difficulty, Mama found a bunk bed which she had to share with the little ones and Liesje had a hammock above it. No place at all for Emmy, Ann, and I. We had arrived too late to make a choice, it was full!

Mama was worried of course, but we found out that the dining rooms were still available and that's where we ended up. This meant that we, armed with our grey ship's blankets, could only go to bed after the last dinners were served, which was around 9:00 at night. And it also meant that we had to get up at 5:00 in the morning as the first breakfasts were served at 6:00 A.M. We slept on top and under the hard tables. We had no mattresses. The sleep/dining rooms were full every night. There were over three-thousand repatriating persons onboard, plus the complete crew for this big ship.

Sietse and Kees showed up for the farewells and found us in this crazy mess. We all met on deck to say our good-byes. Sietse was cool and independent. Mama cried. We sisters talked a lot to hide our feelings. To me, Kees had become such a good friend and it is always hard to part from someone close. There were more friends to part from, and altogether it was very busy.

When at long last the ship's horns sounded, it was time for the visitors to leave and that went fast. A lot of hugging and kissing went on, a lot of separating and leaving. I remember I had goosepimples despite the heat of Singapore. This was a final farewell, not only from our friends and loved-ones but also from the tropics, the home we loved and treasured.

Our family stood together at the railing trying to follow Sietse and Kees among the crowds on the quay. Of course we waved and shouted, so did everyone else. The noise was deafening and we kept it up until the big ship slowly pulled away. The distance became wider and wider between us and the boys on the shore.

Good-bye Singapore, good-bye Sietse and Kees, good-bye good friends and good times of freedom! We were leaving the harbor now and the open sea was before us.

A new adventure.

Gradually everyone relaxed and soon dinner gongs sounded. I must say, it was rather well organized, as room by room, hold by hold, deck by deck the passengers dined. We girls ate mostly last because we were the dining room-sleepers. The food was good and sufficient but we could not always eat together as a family because of our different placings onboard.

Papa and Ids moved quite a few times out of the overcrowded ship's front hold. They tried sleeping on the deck, but the sailors started scrubbing and rinsing it early in the morning, so that was out, of course. Then they tried the stage of one of the lounges, but there a priest started a very early morning mass. It took quite a while till they found a regular spot.

After a couple of days we could leave our backpacks under Mama's bunk bed so that we did not have to drag them along any more. We were all poor and had nothing of value, so that we did not have to be afraid of theft. We pitied Mama and the little ones though, as it was so hot and stuffy sleeping under the decks.

We all had to do chores for the kitchens, mostly peeling potatoes, but we also had to take turns cleaning the toilets and sweeping and washing the diningroom floors. In a way it was good to keep busy and we met a lot of young people who were mostly in a good mood. We had a lot of fun. One good friend was Rita, who had a boyfriend among Sietse's team of airmen. Eventually she married him. She was such a cheerful person, full of ideas of what to do on a crowded ship. We had a marvelous time laughing and giggling, which we had not done for so long. At night we watched shows in the lounges and walked the decks to get some exercise. As a family we usually met in a lounge or on a shaded spot on deck. Papa and Mama were more relaxed also.

After we had traveled a couple of days, something happened which worried us a bit. The little ones, Peter and Elly, came down with a case of the mumps just as we dropped anchor near Colombo, the main harbor of Ceylon. Persons with contagious illnesses would actually have to leave the ship as it could spread and cause an epidemic, but we kept the children isolated in their beds and took turns staying with them. It would have been fatal for Papa if we had to leave the ship now, stay in Colombo with our family, and suffer through another delay. He was already so weak. Luckily it was not discovered and there also were no other cases as far as I recall. Some of us were still troubled with the "monkeypox" but there was a clinic and a hospital ward onboard. Papa particularly was a regular patient in the clinic.

The big ship steamed on and we found ourselves staring over the Indian Ocean, no land around, just water and sky. Peter and Elly were especially delighted watching the flying fish. The cool sea air and the unbelievable sunsets made us feel as if we were on a luxury cruise. And the temperature was still tropical. We enjoyed our trip.

After a good week of only water all around, the *Alcantara* brought us into the Gulf of Aden and, by the Strait of Bab el Mandeb, we entered the Red Sea. It was still very hot in this part of the world, even if the cool sea winds helped to keep us comfortable. But gradually we felt the air cooling off even more and it became definitely colder the farther the ship steamed up into the Red Sea. We each only had a couple of pairs of shorts and one dress, no socks and just sandals, so we froze. The change was so dramatic that people developed colds and flus and all of a sudden the hospital was full and the sickbays had to be extended. Our little Peter caught such a bad cold and cough that he entered the children's section of the hospital. First it had been so hot and now it had become so draughty and chilly in the large hold. There was no heat but human body heat. We had only one thin grey ship's blanket per person.

By the middle of February we dropped anchor at Suez. Every family or couple or single person received food stamp

cards and registration permits and not very long after the
distribution of the paperwork, little boats appeared alongside our ship. We were told we would receive winter clothes
in Ataka, a little place in Egypt. We went down the little
ladders into the boats and were taken ashore at Ataka. Here
a miniature train was waiting to take us for a short ride
through the desert and when it stopped we heard music
playing. A couple of long barracks stood in the middle of
nowhere. We were shown inside. There were all kinds of
flags waving in the soft winds. There was a babysitting service. Little tables were set up with refreshments and treats
for everyone. We could sit down in garden chairs and feast
ourselves on buns with Dutch cheeses, cakes, cookies, and
all kinds of fruits. It was fantastic. All this was set up by the
Red Cross and some charitable institutions. We couldn't believe our eyes!

After that we could choose our winter clothes. There
were racks and racks full of them. Mama was in full action.
She chose clothes for the little ones first while we waited at
the food area. Then we all went in to the different size-sec-
tions to choose ours. It was so much fun but also difficult.
We had no idea what to wear in a cold country and here
Mama came in with advice. We got underwear, slips, pyjamas, socks, shoes, a dress or blouse and skirt, hat, scarf, and
mitts. I think I took a blouse and skirt. At the end of the
row, a winter coat. Mine was a deep blue herringbone material. Emmy and Ann had bright red ones, not exactly their
choice but they ran out of coats. They were warm and that
was most important. In a side booth we received a little
package with toothpaste, brush and soap and at the very
end of the barrack an extra gift, a make-up kit. What an ex-
citement, smiling faces everywhere. The adults and young

people received a sturdy bag to take the clothes on board and the children a smaller one. It worked out perfectly.

Back on our ship we realized how good it had been to set foot ashore again. It was such a break on this long trip. We found it hard to store all these new bags full of new clothes, there was so little space. Under Mama's bed it looked like a warehouse. The coats particularly took up a lot of space.

We stayed anchored for a few days because it took time for so many people to be supplied with clothes. Papa did not get a suit, there was nothing available any more. He only received an overcoat and that was good as the weather deteriorated fast, very strangely. You could see the difference on board, everyone was better dressed, the children especially showed off their new clothes. Peter had not been able to come as he was still cooped up in the hospital, but we had sneaked some goodies for him with us, which pleased him immensely.

During our time in Singapore we had not even thought about winter clothes. I remember I chose a peach-colored pair of pyjamas of very fine flannelette. I took the pyjama top, hand-sewed some cuffs on the long sleeves, and wore it as a blouse. I received a lot of compliments on my pretty blouse. We became very inventive during our "nothing" years and could do wonders with little things.

When finally everyone was back on board, the large ship started moving again into the last stretch of the Red Sea. And then there was the Suez Canal. We slowed down. Such an immense ship cannot move quickly through a relatively narrow but deep canal so as not to damage the shores. A couple of small pilot boats went ahead of our ship, perhaps to ensure a safe crossing. We entered the canal early in the morning. Papa had said the night before that we should take it all in, as possibly this would be our last trip ever through the canal. We sat or stood therefore all day watching the sights. The desert on one side and here and there some greening and some buildings on the other side. Interesting but not beautiful. About halfway down, the canal widened into a couple of lakes, the Bitter and the Timsah lakes. It was slightly greener around the lakes but right behind them was sand and more sand. We also saw a few Bedouins with their camels.

It was a long day and the further we traveled the colder it became. This was very unusual we were told and when the ship reached Port Said, the first city at the end of the canal, the Arabs stood on the quay trampling and stamping their bare feet. They had their robes wrapped tightly around their bodies. It was colder than it had been in one hundred years. It soon became dark but we wanted to see the arrival in Port Said. That night I wore my new winter coat. And I was wondering if I would be able to stand the cold weather in the country of Holland.

Twenty-Four

On the *Alcantara* to Holland

As USUAL we were up at the crack of dawn. Papa had warned us to come up on deck right after breakfast to take advantage of the time our ship would be in Port Said. And yes, we soon understood what he meant. We could not go ashore, but we were able to enjoy the antics of the multitude of little boats that, so early, had gathered around our ship. They were carrying merchandise like woodcarvings, leather ware, porcelain, handicrafts, shells and artwork made with shells and much more.

We were in awe how the deals were made with the passengers on the ship. After the price for a desired item was set by bartering and by holding up of fingers of "how much," a basket on a double rope carried the purchased item up to the customer on deck and then the money was returned in the same basket. Not many people cheated this way, it all went in good faith.

Some merchants even tried to please the customers by speaking some words in the language spoken on the ship. And there was one man in particular who kept on calling out loud, "Abram, Levi, David, *wat koop je?*" (what do you buy?). We cheered him on, it was so funny.

Papa spoilt us all. With my twenty-first birthday coming up in a couple of days, he bought me a beautiful deep blue leather handbag, to go with my blue winter coat. I was so pleased. I still have the purse. Emmy, Ann, and Liesje could choose something also, but I have forgotten what they got. The others, Ids, Peter, and Elly were excited too with their gifts. I know the little ones got something made of shells and Ids a leather wallet. We all had such a good time.

There were also divers who fished up any coin that was dropped into the dirty harbor water. These men and boys were fantastic! They dived from the tiniest miniature boats and some of them stayed under water purposely for the longest time. When they surfaced to receive an applause from the passengers, they always showed the coin between their teeth. It was still very cold that day and their bare bodies were shivering violently. Their puny little boats looked like floating coconut shells to us on top of the high deck. It was amazing how they could find their boats again after their dives. One of them even dove right under our ship and came up on the other side. He must have had a double set of lungs! For us on the decks it was another marvelous diversion on this crowded ship.

Dark, rainy, and stormy weather awaited us when we entered the Mediterranean Sea. It turned out to be quite a severe storm, which would last all through that southern European sea. The *Alcantara* developed a definite sway which made lots and lots of people very seasick. I don't know why, but it did not affect my family. None of us had to go down with it. The dining rooms were quite empty, but our family was there. Emmy, Ann, and I usually dined together and one stormy night at a dinner which was served by the repatriating British P.O.W.s, we had Christmas plum pudding with rum sauce for dessert. I have no idea why but it tasted extra good and while we were digging into this treat, the soldiers made the comment, "And the sisters, they eat and eat!" They stood there laughing at us. We had practiced a lot of English in Singapore so we answered, "Why not, we are not seasick." This broke the ice and as it was not busy at all in the dining room, they sat down with us and continued to tease us. Nobody mentioned the war.

I did not like this cold weather. Rain, yes, I had been used to the tropical downpours, but this cold wind with the driving rain was so different. It was no wonder that a call came over the intercom for volunteers to report in the sickbay. Emmy and I went to help out.

Most of the assistant nurses and even doctors were sick with this strange illness which only shows up on ships and boats. I found my friend Rita in bed also. She was still smiling but very sourly and she could not understand why the storm did not affect us. She had been volunteering in the hospital from the beginning of our trip. "And now," she said, "that everyone needs me most, I can't help." The poor girl. Emmy and I had to help out in the men's measles bay. My goodness, these people were sick! Their weakened bodies had no resistance and now they had contracted this children's illness. It made them dreadfully sick. They were burning up with fever, had big sores around their mouths and eyes and maybe the seasickness influenced them also? They were suffering. We had to freshen the cloths on their foreheads and help them drink some water or juices. There was so much to do. We thanked the Lord that we were so healthy. There was also a young man who had been seasick from the moment he set foot on board. He was skin and bones and said he wished he was back in the camps again where at least he could eat whatever there was to eat. "Now," he said, "I am dying." Papa had mentioned a fellow in his hold in the beginning who was so very seasick. As soon as he was off the ship he was fine, for example when he was getting clothes in Ataka. But he had to endure it a little longer till we reached Holland.

After the storm subsided Emmy and I kept our occasional shifts. There was a lot to learn from human misery. By the time this storm was over we had almost reached the Strait of Gibraltar. It was still very windy and quite cold but we watched the big rock, another milestone. As soon as we were north of Spain the conversations on board spun more and more around the arrival in Holland. Everyone seemed happy that the end of our voyage was in sight. It was not all that comfortable on board and most women and children were separated from husbands and fathers which put the responsibility again on the mothers. Questions also arose among us young people what it would be like to be free in a strange country. We silently worried about it.

The further north we moved, the colder it became. We wore our winter clothes all the time by now. It became foggier and rainier every day, even to the point that the fog horns sounded, which was an eerie noise in this ghostly world. It was almost March, 1946, winter in Europe.

Was this what we could expect? Maybe in a warm living room it would not be so depressing. Lots of people were sniffling and sneezing with colds and everyone shivered practically all day long. There was no heating system on board except the human heat created by so many people. Peter and Elly also had permanent colds. Mama did not know how to protect her chickens enough. She still had high expectations for her family. She kept on talking about her Holland and we did not want to disappoint her. What did we know about it but for the maps in the schoolbooks before the war?

However, we were not in Holland yet. The *Alcantara* docked in Southampton, England on the first of March and stayed there. What now? They told us that a Dutch ship would be sent to transport all the Dutch P.O.W.s, women and children also, back to Holland in two trips. But first all the British P.O.W.s left the ship.

It was still very foggy and raining when we docked. The music was playing and big welcoming signs were up on the quay to receive the boys and men home. We saw families welcoming fathers back and there were a lot of teary eyes and smiling faces. It made us anxious to get off the ship also. By watching the festivities on the shore, we had not noticed the arrival of the Dutch ship, the *Sibajak*. It had come alongside the *Alcantara* on the other side. That same day the first half of our passengers transferred onto it plus the sick and a lot of luggage. They used a bridge-type gangplank to just walk over onto the other ship as the smaller *Sibajak* lay much lower in the water. I assume that the passenger selection was done alphabetically because our family name started with a *T* and we were listed in the second shipment. When the *Sibajak* departed they received a loud and whistling exit from the remaining "Alcantarians."

It became quite a bit calmer and roomier onboard after the first load had left. It took the *Sibajak* four days to return. In the meantime, we could not go ashore as nobody had passports. So we watched the dock workers do their jobs and we started to realize that we were entering a new world where everyone does his own thing. No *babus*, no *katjongs*, no *kebons*, no *kokkies* here, although they were a necessity in the Indies. Now we certainly were among the poor, we had nothing but each other. During the last five years we had not been spoiled with servants and had definitely learned to pack our own bags. Papa and Mama had always taught us to respect our servants for what they were and treat them as human beings. They also had been happy with us, I knew that. All these thoughts went through my head while we were waiting on the chilly ship for the return of the *Sibajak*.

It was still misty and overcast when we slowly steamed up the North Sea. At least it was not raining and the sun came out the next day. It was either the 6th or the 7th of March, 1946. We were now on a warm ship. Warm lounges, warm cabins, clean sheets and double blankets, good Dutch meals and everyone spoke our language. It was soothing to our feelings and we assumed ourselves to be on Dutch soil already. It was the same ship, the *Sibajak*, we had traveled on when Papa had his furlough and we as children had been very much smaller. I will always remember the warmth of it because those four days in Southampton had really chilled me.

We steamed up the North Sea Canal to Amsterdam and I had a strange sense of homecoming this way. When the *Sibajak* docked, they soon started with the debarkation. There were long lines, there were officials welcoming us. I said good-bye to Rita, who was also on this second trip and we promised to write, which we still do!

I don't remember if there was music. It all seemed very "matter of fact" to these welcoming committees. So many had come back ahead of us already, but it went very smoothly.

Eight Prison Camps

Someone was assigned to our family. He took us to a minibus. As there were nine of us and almost all were adult size, we needed this kind of transportation. The man drove us to Papa and Mama's home town, Dokkum, in the north of Holland. We made one stop for lunch in a small town. Then we were "home." One thing I regret. Kees gave me his air force cap as a souvenir when we parted in Singapore. I had worn it all through our voyage. Then I left it in the minibus and I never got it back!

Twenty-Five

We Arrived

Now you'll probably wonder what happened to me and my family after we came "home." Did we live happily ever after? Were there castles and princes waiting to make it all better? Well, it was all strange, strange, strange. We were happy to be away from the war scenes. I particularly was so happy to be free. Free from fear, from anxiety, from mistreatment. We were grateful to be in Holland, but . . . ! Isn't there a "but" everywhere?

We arrived in a small town with friendly folks, we made lots of friends, had boyfriends too. *But* the understanding of what we went through was missing. They had it so bad during "their" war, that we did not talk about "ours." In Papa and Mama's hometown, just before the liberation in May of 1945, about twenty, mostly young, men from the town and surrounding villages had been executed by the Germans in retaliation for the approaching Allied troops. This had been a terribly cruel act, of course. It had happened just outside town. And although it had been a horrendous fright in town, during the actual war years not very many serious things had happened. Everyone lived in his own home, had his own furniture, his own bed to sleep in. Schools had been on, churches had been functioning on a normal basis. There had been no serious undernourishment, though there had been restrictions. All in all, in the northern provinces life had been pretty regular compared to other parts of central and east Holland, where definitely many scary things had happened. That's why we felt that their situation could not be compared with ours at all.

When in early March, 1946, our minivan sped over the roads of Holland heading for Dokkum, we were still unaware of all this. Everything was bare and bleak. It was winter. There were some patches of snow here and there. This kind of landscape especially was new to me. There were no leaves on the trees and I noticed the low flat views of the countryside. The "low lands," that is Holland! Quite a difference from where we had come.

We stopped once in Zwolle, which was a small town about halfway, for soup and nice Dutch buns with cheese. Then we sped on to Friesland, one of the northern provinces. We arrived in Dokkum in the afternoon at Opa and Grootmoe's house on the Ooster Singel. It was a small place right on the street, under the same roof as the neighbors. Everything was so small and narrow in town when we entered it. Even when we had stopped in Zwolle, the streets seemed so short and narrow. Instead of asphalt, most streets were paved with bricks or cobblestones, particularly in the smaller towns and villages. We sure would have to get used to this pattern, although it gave us a very rustic impression of an old country.

Quite a large part of the family was present. Mama's sister Anna with three of their children, Papa's mother, our

Beppe, was there. His father, our Pake, had passed away. Then there was Papa's oldest brother and his wife with several of their offspring. I don't know what we did when the first greetings were over. There were tears and smiles. It was terribly crowded in the small living room which had a particular smell, not bad, but so peculiarly Dutch that I have never forgotten it.

I remember I was glad that we had arrived, but I also felt lost. We had no place to go. We had no say in where we were going to stay. It was all arranged, which was good in some ways, but I sensed the uncertainty of no control. We had nothing, we were nothing, we knew nothing, compared to all these people who had sorted everything out. I don't want to sound ungrateful, but we were treated as my description. After all, I was 21 and I had accomplished nothing. But because of our family's optimistic views, we eventually managed very well.

And again we were separated. Papa and Mama stayed at Opa and Grootmoe's with the little ones and Liesje. There were ladder-like stairs to go up to the second floor. How they all slept there, I have no idea as the upstairs was so tiny. But it was shiny clean. Ids went with Oom (Uncle) Onne and Tante (Aunt) Wiets where he learned to walk on wooden shoes. He had no problem with them. I could never walk in them. He once even kept them on in their house while he walked up to the dining room table. Tante Wiets hastily told him that wooden shoes stay outside and that you come in in your socks only.

Ann and I went with Tante Anne and Oom Reinder to the bakery. Emmy stayed with Beppe as she was her namesake. Beppe still lived in the same house on the river Ee where Papa had grown up.

Eight Prison Camps

In Tante Anne's house it smelled deliciously like freshly baked bread and pastries. The first freshly baked bread was unforgettable. Tante Anne had a peculiar way of slicing bread sideways which always fascinated me. She started normally at the crust at one end of the loaf, and sliced even slices but she always ended up cutting the last slice almost off the bottom of the loaf. The bread was so tasty and fresh. I was not thinking of gaining weight as yet because we were all still pretty slim. But all that bread and the rich food of Friesland had to be watched.

Ann and I had to sleep in a bedstead in the hardly ever used living room. They called that room the *mooie kamer*, the nice room. Only when church officials visited or on birthdays, the open hearth was lit. The bedstead was never used as the family had their bedrooms upstairs, nice and dry, right over the warm ovens of the bakery. So this bedstead was chilly and cold to the point of feeling damp. There was no heat in the room when we slept there. And even if Tante Anne put a "hot rock" in the bed which had been heated up in the ovens of the bakery, our thin tropical blood did not want to warm up. Boy, was it cold in that cave-like bedstead! We had enough blankets though, but we slept with our socks on and in flannelette pajamas, to no avail. We never slept warm while there.

Luckily Papa found a temporary house for us all within a week. The manse of the church stood empty as there was a vacancy. We had just moved in there when our whole family came down with a terrible itch which turned out to be scabies. Apparently we had all contracted it from the grey ships blankets on board the *Alcantara*. These blankets were never cleaned. One night covered with a smelly sulphur ointment cured us all. Our nightclothes had to be destroyed and all other clothes had to be laundered in the hottest suds, but we got rid of it. Better food, especially fresh fruits and vegetables did the rest. Mama hauled in little boxes of oranges and tomatoes for our large family. Slowly our boils disappeared, our tiredness changed to more energy, our systems cleared themselves of all the dirt we had to consume during the past war years. However, more than a year later little Peter still had to undergo a cure for internal worms, which he did not seem to be able to get rid of. Also symptoms of the beriberi and edemas cropped up after many years of good food and comfortable living.

Meanwhile, our cousins introduced us to some of their friends, but it did not click. We stayed loners for quite a while and always spent time with each other. When my sisters and I walked through town, we felt we were being stared at. Later we heard from good friends that, because of our colorful coats we had been called "The Wise Ones from the East." We did not grasp the sarcasm of it at that time. We were in a way very ignorant and innocent, not able to believe that in a free land people could think that way. But then, they did not know what had happened to us and did not understand our feelings.

In one of the first weeks we visited an exhibition of war-happenings in the Netherlands. As we did not know anything about what had taken place during the war in Holland, we were very interested. We watched how they hid important persons and Jews from the Germans and learned how the underground activities had been organized. We had gone with our cousins and some newly-made friends. Affected by the impact of what we saw, we volunteered some of our own experiences but to our surprise our friends looked at us as if we had made up our stories. They did not even comment or ask questions. Right away they started telling us of how they had to eat tulip bulbs and sugar beets because of food shortages. We would have liked to eat anything like that if it just had been there, but for us there was nothing! But we were not out to "boast" about who had experienced the worst of the war. We just kept quiet as nobody listened to us. When we mentioned it at home, Papa and Mama advised us to leave it, to go on with our lives, which we did. But deep down I was at a loss about such blindness on the part of the people who were supposed to be our own.

We were happy to live in a real house again, together as a family. We did not have any furniture, so we went to the greengrocer and borrowed some orange crates to sit on around the one and only kitchen table in the house, which we had placed in the dining room. Papa and Mama borrowed an armchair and a small easy chair out of the *mooie kamer* from Tante Anne and Oom Reinder with a promise to return them when we would get our own!

Papa acquired some money, I don't know how. He also went to the H.A.R.K. office (Help Action Red Cross). This place offered some help to repatriated people from the Indies. We got beds, mattresses, and blankets. There were sheets too and gradually we furnished the house with the most necessary items. There were no drapes over the windows. The sidewalk in the narrow street ran right by them, so everyone could look inside. Soon the gossip went through town that "These yellow looking Indians are so strange and so different. They are sitting on wooden crates around a bare kitchen table, drinking from tin cans." Those were our camp mugs. When we, one way or another, heard these stories we laughed about it. Several friends had asked us on occasion why we looked so yellow, but we had not even realized that we looked that way to others. Most people from the tropics acquire this slightly yellow-looking skin color. It was very hard to convince the town folks that we were survivors of a terrible war. They had no idea, but our sense of humor prevailed. We all enjoyed being together as a family in a house. We were free! Only later we realized how cruel people can be.

Nobody in town had lost anything materially and there was also nobody who offered us anything to get back on our feet. But maybe they had donated things to different funds, I don't know. Papa and Mama had to provide for all of us and they did. One day, sure enough, Papa came home glowing. There had been a complete dining room set at the Red Cross Center with eight matching chairs. We were rich! We could sit on a chair to eat our meals, read the paper, write letters, and so forth. It was fantastic. We used this set for as long as I was in Holland. Much later Mama bought a new set.

When we were in Suez, Ataka, where we received our winter clothes, we had also received food and clothing stamps (textile coupons). Papa did not receive a suit or anything like it and it became time to see to that. So, Papa and Mama went to a well known men's store where they explained what was required. The owner of the store greeted them and left a staff member with them for service. The man turned out to be very uncooperative. Papa was told that there was nothing available and he had no idea when anything would come in. Sorry! When they left they had the distinct feeling that they were mistrusted and suspected of not being able to pay for the merchandise. It was a very insulting visit. Papa and Mama marched right on to another clothing store. This store owner did not belong to our church but he was well known. Here Papa was treated quite the opposite. They tried everything to please Papa and after a couple of weeks he received a very reasonable suit of good quality and fit. This second store sold numerous coats and outfits to our family in the coming years.

I took a sewing course at a vocational school. From then on I sewed most of the clothes for our family. In this way we could save up for other necessary items in our household. Until Papa started working again we had to be very careful how we spent money. I believe that there was a fund from which we received assistance for a while. So gradually we became used to living in a house again, in a town, in a different country. We all tried our best to go on with our lives and to forget the past years. I had a hard time getting used to the mentality of the town folks. We only talked about the war years when we were together as a family. The memories lived on deep down inside of us, never forgotten. And we did not turn out so bad.

Twenty-Six

It Never Ended

OF COURSE everyone in my family went back to school, except me. School: that was quite an adaptation for everyone. To sit at a desk all day instead of doing what you wanted to do. Quite a change!

The little ones went right into the grade for their age. The older ones were all four years behind, but they still started in the grade closest to their age groups. With some tutoring they managed, although there were some hectic moments with homework and classmates. Friends came pouring into our house and we all joined sports clubs for swimming and athletics. Soon we singled out some friends who were sincere and fun to be with. Still, we hardly ever discussed the years in the camps.

After a couple of months Sietse returned from the Indies. By then we had already moved to a large old house, as the manse was going to be occupied again by a newly called minister. During the German occupation Sietse had continued his studies at the technical college in the capital of Friesland. Nothing went drastically wrong until the last school year when, just before the end, an order came from the Germans that after the final exams, all these young men had to report for work in the German factories. So, the exams were moved up and most of the boys went undercover. What the Germans did I don't know, but for the rest of the war Sietse disappeared. He moved around from family to family and as soon as it was over he tried to find his own family in the Indies.

Well, when his battalion was finally sent on to Batavia from Singapore, they never became involved in any military action except for standing guard. In the air force there was not much to do and soon the decision was made to send these boys back to Holland, as most of them had been volunteers anyway. Sietse came home and again we were all excited. But he had nothing to do. It was different somehow. He became restless and the main reason for that was perhaps that he had been away from home so long, he could not adjust very well to family life. He decided to join a training school near Amsterdam to become a flyer. That had always been his purpose in life. And so it happened. He was very good. Not very long afterwards he went solo and after he completed the required flying hours he graduated and was hired by K.L.M. Airlines. He stayed with this company until he retired. He, of course, flew to practically every country in the world and piloted the 747s. We were all very proud of him. His wife stayed with him if he was stationed in another country for some time, but when his two children started school, they settled in Holland, in a home not far from the Amsterdam airport, Schiphol. His son followed in his father's footsteps and now also flies all over the world.

Now back to the scholars. Ids in particular, had a hard time at school. He had been finishing grade four before the war and was now placed in the second grade of high school at age 15. He often came home, threw his books in a corner and muttered, "I'm just dumb, I don't know anything, I think I'll quit!" He was so frustrated. A sympathetic teacher regularly helped him after school and as far as I know, Ids did amazingly well. But he was the tallest and oldest boy in his grade and when he turned 17 he decided he was going to join the Royal Dutch Marines. Mama was heavily against it, but Papa understood what Ids had been going through and supported him. Ids left for Amsterdam. We missed him. There was an empty spot in our family.

At the Marine Academy he was tested and did remarkably well. He acquired his high school diploma and continued his studies in radio radar mechanics for the marines, for which he eventually earned a degree. He served over all the world's seas, from Amsterdam to Argentina to Asia. He found a lovely girl in Amsterdam and made her his wife. Two children were born while he was out somewhere in the world on a wavy ocean; for the third he could luckily be at home. Later he became a teacher at the Seafarers' school in Amsterdam. He was very much admired by his peers. At age thirty he became the youngest major ever in the history of the Royal Dutch Marines. He earned this title mainly because since he started with the marines, his conduct had been spotless. He was honored with a medal and a big celebration. We were all so proud of him. Physically Ids always seemed healthy but several times he had to have surgery on his intestines. He was able to retire early since he had started with the Marines early. He enjoys his retirement thoroughly with his wife and children and grandchildren.

Emmy, Ann, and Liesje did very well at school. Emmy and Liesje went to Teachers' College after high school. They taught for years, married, and continued in the educational field. Emmy was pretty healthy, nothing happened to her that would not happen to any other growing woman. She also married and had four children, a very happy family. Liesje however, suffered a setback in her life which was definitely a result of the prison camps. After she married she found out that she would never enjoy motherhood. As she entered the camps at age eight, almost four years of malnutrition caused her body to be underdeveloped. These are just the years when a girl grows into puberty. Although outwardly she looked a healthy girl, her womb could never produce children. It became a great sorrow in her and her husband's life as they traveled from one specialist to another. A couple of years later they adopted a beautiful girl who became the light of their lives. But our whole family understood and felt her grief.

Emmy and her husband are both retired now and are enjoying travel and recreation. Lies and her husband also retired recently. They too travel a lot. They all live in their own homes in Holland.

Ann finished a five year H.B.S. and went to work in several hospitals as an x-ray technician. She learned a lot and enjoyed her stay in the hospital dorm with all her companions. She eventually married and moved to Canada where she and her husband went through the usual difficult first years after immigration. But it gradually became better. She still suffers from frightening nightmares about the camps and does not want to discuss the past. But she and her husband are both happily retired and enjoy their grandchildren.

Papa started working again as a teacher as soon as he felt somewhat better. His main complaint was that the Dutch school children were quite the opposite from the native children of his school in Solo. Here they were rowdy, loud, and disobedient. It was not easy for Papa to start from the bottom up. He always felt very tired for the rest of his life. He bicycled to his schools winter and summer, every day until his retirement at age 65.

The house we had moved into was cold and damp and had a terribly leaky roof. Mama and I went upstairs to clean and make the beds with mitts and heavy sweaters on. Our thin tropical blood took a long time to heat up. Papa made plans to have a brand new house built in a much better neighborhood. He definitely ventured out and bravely attacked all odds. Papa was the best father a child could wish for. He supported each one of us with his or her problems, with career choices, with moral sustenance. Four times he tried to return to the Indies. He went through rigorous medical testing and failed them every time. It saddened him forever that he could not continue his life's work. He established a happy home for us all. Luckily he saw all his children happily married and even visited Ann and me in Canada. Papa should have retired sooner but he was working for a better retirement income for himself and Mama. He only enjoyed it for five years. His tired body gave way and he passed away completely spent, definitely a result of the war years in the prison camps, from which he never really recovered.

I lived for two years in the newly built house before I moved to Canada with my husband. It was marvelous, in the new house, as for the first time we had a real washroom and shower since we came to Holland. I always stayed home to help Mama with our large family when everyone went back to school. I know how to keep house, how to cook and clean. Papa helped me find the right evening business college so that I eventually would be able to find a secretarial position. I did this and studied shorthand, typing, and business correspondence and knowledge. I also studied English on my own and read English books. I did secretarial work for a year at the office of a dairy factory. But when Mama could not handle her workload any longer, I came home again. That was a difficult time for me as I was engaged by then and my fiancé and I were trying to save up for our future. My income was gone and even if Papa and Mama compensated me somewhat, I knew they could not afford to pay me. We sent for our emigration papers and soon after our wedding we left for Canada, much to Mama's sorrow. But it was very hard to find a good position in Holland. I don't think that I kept any medical problems resulting from our internment. Swollen feet and hands appeared for a long time as an aftermath of the beriberi or edema, but eventually this disappeared. My husband and I went through difficult immigrant years in Canada. Even with him I hardly ever spoke about our past war years, while in the meantime I heard everything about the European war. I became a widow at forty-three when my husband passed away from a heart attack. We had three teenagers at the time but here my secretarial training came in handy. I was retrained in the more updated business world and started working for a government department. I did this for approximately twenty years and now enjoy, I think, a well-deserved retirement.

The little ones also grew up and completely emersed themselves in the town's life. After I went to Canada, when they were ten and eleven, I kept in close contact with our family by mail, but I missed seeing them grow up. Elly grew into a tall slim girl who was always optimistic and cheerful. Right after we had come back to Holland, the doctor had diagnosed her with rickets, which continued to bother her while she was growing up. She also became a teacher and was, and still is, born for the job. She married and had three children, but she herself suffered a lot with her back and she always has a sore throat. She had her tonsils removed after she had her third baby but still continues to suffer with her throat and back. But her sunny nature keeps her on top of things. Her letters look like an old-fashioned raisin bread, always full of news. I believe that because of our close family life and Christian upbringing, none of us has kept mental scars resulting from the concentration camps.

Peter grew up into a tall, athletic young man, seemingly without many problems. At age 19 he also moved to Canada, which almost broke Mama's heart. The "little ones" were not so little anymore, but they had stayed at home for the longest time. They had the best of everything as, of course, the rest of the family had left home and it all became easier for Papa and Mama. Peter worked in several hospitals in Canada as an oxygen-therapist. He married and when they had three children they moved to New Zealand, mainly because they hated shovelling snow, or so they said. We missed them here in Canada and hated to see them leave. While in that faraway land, Peter contracted an incurable disease. He has been fighting it for many years. His hobby and interest as a ham-radio operator has kept him optimistic and courageous. He has many friends all over the world, but it has been very hard on his family. Luckily they all still live around him so that he is not completely alone. If this illness is a result of the concentration camps it is not established. We all hope that a cure may be found.

And now Mama, our heroine. She thrived in her hometown. She recovered well from the stress and anxiety about

Eight Prison Camps

us all. She made sure that we all received the life we were entitled to. We are grateful for her courage and willpower and I think many of her children have inherited it. Mama lived a long happy life even after Papa died. Papa spoiled her continuously after the war. She saw all her grandchildren grow up. She visited us here in Canada many, many times and she even traveled all alone to New Zealand to see Peter and his family. She held several great-grandchildren in her arms. She was a brave woman. At almost 86 she passed away from a sudden tumor. Her faith and trust in the Lord was her only peace. We all will miss her forever!

And now that our family is getting on, there is a point I want to make. I wrote this story because it was never told. It was never acknowledged; now it is known to the world. I sincerely hope that whoever reads my story may learn that hate destroys, that wars should not be fought, they should be *prevented*. Even if my family did not suffer from terrible traumas, I have come to know many who outlived the concentration camps but who are to this day still suffering from ailments and psychological aftereffects of that horrendous time under the Japanese. Wherever we live on this planet, we will observe cruelty, envy, hunger, thirst, humiliation, fear, and darkness. I experienced it all and the memory will always stay with me. And even if God did not always seem to be there with us in the camps when we were so forlorn, we kept our faith. We hoped, we loved and, through prayer, we became survivors in our weakest hours.

Glossary

Dutch

B.P.M. Bataafse Petroleum Maatschappij	Batavia Oil Company
Batavia	Jakarta
beppe	grandma (Frisian)
Brille-Jap	Spectacles-Jap
Dokkum	Town in N. Friesland, Netherlands
Gordel van Smaragd	Emerald Belt
grootmoe	grandmother
Hansje m'n Knecht	Hansel my Slave
H.B.S.	Acronym for *Hogere Burger School*, one of the types of Dutch high schools. It offered a five year college preparation program.
K.N.I.L. Koninklyk Nederlands Indisch Leger	Royal Netherlands Indian Army
oma	granny, grandma
onderwys	education
oom	uncle
oorlog	war
opa	grandpa
pake	grandpa (Frisian)
plastron	A sun top made out of a triangular piece of fabric tied at the neck and waist

stront-ploeg	shit gang
tante	aunt
vel over been	skin on bone
"Wat koop je?"	"What do you buy?"
Zwolle	town in central Holland

JAPANESE

"Dai sanpang to dai sipang, fukumudju idju arimasin."	"Everything on block three and four is in order."
fu-sin-bang	nightwatch
heihoh	native soldier
itji, ni, san, si, goh, roku, sitji, hadji, kju, dju	one, two . . . ten
keimpe tei	military police
keirei	bow
kiwotsuke	attention
naore	at ease
nippon	Japan
"Susu itai fukumu ita imas."	"We pass you onto the next block."

MALAY

Ambarawa	mountain town in the center of mid Java
anglo	small earthenware barbeque
babu	female household help

Glossary

bagus	nice
bale-bale	wooden board to sleep on
Bandung (Dutch spelling)	large city on mountain plateau in southwest Java
Banjubiru	small village above Ambarawa
barang	luggage
Blandas	Indonesian term for Europeans
coolie	native laborer
dessa	rural village
djati hout	hard wood, compares to teak
djeruk	Mandarin
emper	covered open gallery
gedek	sheets of woven bamboo slats
grobak	oxen drawn cart
gudang	storeroom
gulah jawa	clumps of dark brown sugar derived from sugar cane
heiho	native soldier recruited by the Japanese, also called sticks army
indo	offspring of (usually) Dutch family and native
"Itu saya."	"That is mine."
Java	Main island of Indonesia
Jogjakarta	a city 60 kilometers southwest of Surakarta
kali	river
kampong	native section in town or village
kapok	kapok (mattress stuffing) grows like cotton in seed pods
katjong	young boy, temporary help
kawat	barbed wire
kebon	gardenhouse worker

kedelee	native-grown hard bean
kembang spatu	shoe flower, hibiscus
keree	bamboo roll curtain
klabang	centipede
klambu	mosquito net
kokki	cook
lekas	fast
mandi	bath
mangku	princely nobleman
merdeka	independence
Muntilan	small village on slopes of the volcano Merapi above Jogjakarta, mid Java
nasi goreng	fried rice
paddi	rice plant
passar	open market place
patjol	broad sided pick
"Pigih"	"Go away!"
poh-poh	diaper
rampok	an armed attack
Romushas	Native slave laborers
sambal	hot red pepper paste
sapu lidih	long broom of bamboo strips
sayur (sayor)	spiced vegetable, meat, or seafood dish
Semarang	harbor city on northern coast of mid Java
slokan	ditch, used as latrine
Suabaya	large harbor city in East Java
Sumowono	mountain village in mid Java
sunan	sultan
Surakarta (Solo)	city in center of mid Java
tangsih	military or police compound
tawar	to bargain

tekleks	wooden sandals, flip-flops
"tida boleh"	"You can't do that!"
tiker	thin woven bamboo mat
Tjilatjap (Cilacap)	Harbor city on the southern coast of central Java
tjit–tjaks	little wall salamanders
"Tulung"	"Help!"
tokeh	large frog-like salamander
toko	shop, store

Monographs in International Studies

Titles Available from Ohio University Press, 1996

Southeast Asia Series

No. 56 **Duiker, William J.** Vietnam Since the Fall of Saigon. 1989. Updated ed. 401 pp. Paper 0-89680-162-4 $20.00.

No. 64 **Dardjowidjojo, Soenjono.** Vocabulary Building in Indonesian: An Advanced Reader. 1984. 664 pp. Paper 0-89680-118-7 $30.00.

No. 65 **Errington, J. Joseph.** Language and Social Change in Java: Linguistic Reflexes of Modernization in a Traditional Royal Polity. 1985. 210 pp. Paper 0-89680-120-9 $25.00.

No. 66 **Binh, Tran Tu.** The Red Earth: A Vietnamese Memoir of Life on a Colonial Rubber Plantation. Tr. by John Spragens. 1984. 102 pp. (SEAT*, V. 5) Paper 0-89680-119-5 $11.00.

No. 68 **Syukri, Ibrahim.** History of the Malay Kingdom of Patani. 1985. 135 pp. Paper 0-89680-123-3 $15.00.

No. 69 **Keeler, Ward.** Javanese: A Cultural Approach. 1984. 559 pp. Paper 0-89680-121-7 $25.00.

No. 70 **Wilson, Constance M. and Lucien M. Hanks.** Burma-Thailand Frontier Over Sixteen Decades: Three Descriptive Documents. 1985. 128 pp. Paper 0-89680-124-1 $11.00.

No. 71 **Thomas, Lynn L. and Franz von Benda-Beckmann,** eds. Change and Continuity in Minangkabau: Local, Regional, and Historical Perspec-tives on West Sumatra. 1985. 353 pp. Paper 0-89680-127-6 $16.00.

No. 72 **Reid, Anthony and Oki Akira,** eds. The Japanese Experience in Indonesia: Selected Memoirs of 1942–1945. 1986. 424 pp., 20 illus. (SEAT, V. 6) Paper 0-89680-132-2 $20.00.

No. 74 **McArthur M. S. H.** Report on Brunei in 1904. Introduced and Annotated by A. V. M. Horton. 1987. 297 pp. Paper 0-89680-135-7 $15.00.

* Southeast Asia Translation Project Group

No. 75 **Lockard, Craig A.** From Kampung to City: A Social History of Kuching, Malaysia, 1820–1970. 1987. 325 pp. Paper 0-89680-136-5 $20.00.

No. 76 **McGinn, Richard,** ed. Studies in Austronesian Linguistics. 1986. 516 pp. Paper 0-89680-137-3 $20.00.

No. 77 **Muego, Benjamin N.** Spectator Society: The Philippines Under Martial Rule. 1986. 232 pp. Paper 0-89680-138-1 $17.00.

No 79 **Walton, Susan Pratt.** Mode in Javanese Music. 1987. 278 pp. Paper 0-89680-144-6 $15.00.

No. 80 **Nguyen Anh Tuan.** South Vietnam: Trial and Experience. 1987. 477 pp., tables. Paper 0-89680-141-1 $18.00.

No. 82 **Spores, John C.** Running Amok: An Historical Inquiry. 1988. 190 pp. paper 0-89680-140-3 $13.00.

No. 83 **Malaka, Tan.** From Jail to Jail. Tr. by Helen Jarvis. 1911. 1209 pp., three volumes. (SEAT V. 8) Paper 0-89680-150-0 $55.00.

No. 84 **Devas, Nick, with Brian Binder, Anne Booth, Kenneth Davey, and Roy Kelly.** Financing Local Government in Indonesia. 1989. 360 pp. Paper 0-89680-153-5 $20.00.

No. 85 **Suryadinata, Leo.** Military Ascendancy and Political Culture: A Study of Indonesia's Golkar. 1989. 235 pp., illus., glossary, append., index, bibliog. Paper 0-89680-154-3 $18.00.

No. 86 **Williams, Michael.** Communism, Religion, and Revolt in Banten in the Early Twentieth Century. 1990. 390 pp. Paper 0-89680-155-1 $14.00.

No. 87 **Hudak, Thomas.** The Indigenization of Pali Meters in Thai Poetry. 1990. 247 pp. Paper 0-89680-159-4 $15.00.

No. 88 **Lay, Ma Ma.** Not Out of Hate: A Novel of Burma. Tr. by Margaret Aung-Thwin. Ed. by William Frederick. 1991. 260 pp. (SEAT V. 9) Paper 0-89680-167-5 $20.00.

No. 89 **Anwar, Chairil.** The Voice of the Night: Complete Poetry and Prose of Chairil Anwar. 1992. Revised Edition. Tr. by Burton Raffel. 196 pp. Paper 0-89680-170-5 $20.00.

No. 90 **Hudak, Thomas John,** tr., The Tale of Prince Samuttakote: A Buddhist Epic from Thailand. 1993. 230 pp. Paper 0-89680-174-8 $20.00.

No. 91 **Roskies, D. M.,** ed. Text/Politics in Island Southeast Asia: Essays in Interpretation. 1993. 330 pp. Paper 0-89680-175-6 $25.00.

No. 92 **Schenkhuizen, Marguérite, translated by Lizelot Stout van Balgooy.** Memoirs of an Indo Woman: Twentieth-Century Life in the East Indies and Abroad. 1993. 312 pp. Paper 0-89680-178-0 $25.00.

No. 93   **Salleh, Muhammad Haji.** Beyond the Archipelago: Selected Poems. 1995. 247 pp. Paper 0-89680-181-0 $20.00.

No. 94   **Federspiel, Howard M.** A Dictionary of Indonesian Islam. 1995. 327 pp. Bibliog. Paper 0-89680-182-9 $25.00.

No. 95   **Leary, John.** Violence and the Dream People: The Orang Asli in the Malayan Emergency 1948–1960. 1995. 275 pp. Maps, illus., tables, appendices, bibliog., index. Paper 0-89680-186-1 $22.00.

No. 96   **Lewis, Dianne.** *Jan Compagnie* in the Straits of Malacca 1641–1795. 1995. 176 pp. Map, appendices, bibliog., index. Paper 0-89680-187-x. $18.00.

Africa Series

No. 43   **Harik, Elsa M. and Donald G. Schilling.** The Politics of Education in Colonial Algeria and Kenya. 1984. 102 pp. Paper 0-89680-117-9 $12.50.

No. 45   **Keto, C. Tsehloane.** American-South African Relations 1784–1980: Review and Select Bibliography. 1985. 169 pp. Paper 0-89680-128-4 $11.00.

No. 46   **Burness, Don,** ed. Wanasema: Conversations with African Writers. 1985. 103 pp. paper 0-89680-129-2 $11.00.

No. 47   **Switzer, Les.** Media and Dependency in South Africa: A Case Study of the Press and the Ciskei "Homeland." 1985. 97 pp. Paper 0-89680-130-6 $10.00.

No. 49   **Hart, Ursula Kingsmill.** Two Ladies of Colonial Algeria: The Lives and Times of Aurelie Picard and Isabelle Eberhardt. 1987. 153 pp. paper 0-89680-143-8 $11.00.

No. 51   **Clayton, Anthony and David Killingray.** Khaki and Blue: Military and Police in British Colonial Africa. 1989. 347 pp. Paper 0-89680-147-0 $20.00.

No. 52   **Northrup, David.** Beyond the Bend in the River: African Labor in Eastern Zaire, 1865–1940. 1988. 282 pp. Paper 0-89680-151-9 $15.00.

No. 53   **Makinde, M. Akin.** African Philosophy, Culture, and Traditional Medicine. 1988. 172 pp. Paper 0-89680-152-7 $16.00.

No. 54   **Parson, Jack,** ed. Succession to High Office in Botswana: Three Case Studies. 1990. 455 pp. Paper 0-89680-157-8 $20.00.

No. 56   **Staudinger, Paul.** In the Heart of the Hausa States. Tr. by Johanna E. Moody. Foreword by Paul Lovejoy. 1990. In two volumes., 469 + 224 pp., maps, apps. Paper 0-89680-160-8 (2 vols.) $35.00.

No. 57   **Sikainga, Ahmad Alawad.** The Western Bahr Al-Ghazal under British Rule, 1898–1956. 1991. 195 pp. Paper 0-89680-161-6 $15.00.

No. 58   Wilson, Louis E. The Krobo People of Ghana to 1892: A Political and Social History. 1991. 285 pp. Paper 0-89680-164-0 $20.00.

No. 59   du Toit, Brian M. Cannabis, Alcohol, and the South African Student: Adolescent Drug Use, 1974–1985. 1991. 176 pp., notes, tables. Paper 0-89680-166-7 $17.00.

No. 60   Falola, Toyin and Dennis Itavyar, eds. The Political Economy of Health in Africa. 1992. 258 pp., notes, tables. Paper 0-89680-166-7 $20.00.

No. 61   Kiros, Tedros. Moral Philosophy and Development: The Human Condition in Africa. 1992. 199 pp., notes. Paper 0-89680-171-3 $20.00.

No. 62   Burness, Don. Echoes of the Sunbird: An Anthology of Contemporary African Poetry. 1993. 198 pp. Paper 0-89680-173-x $17.00.

No. 63   Glew, Robert S. and Chaibou Babalé. Hausa Folktales from Niger. 1993. 143 pp. Paper 0-89680-176-4 $15.00.

No. 64   Nelson, Samuel H. Colonialism in the Congo Basin 1880–1940. 1994. 290 pp. Index. Paper 0-89680-180-2 $23.00.

Latin America Series

No. 9   Tata, Robert J. Structural Changes in Puerto Rico's Economy: 1947–1976. 1981. 118 pp. paper 0-89680-107-1 $12.00.

No. 12   Wallace, Brian F. Ownership and Development: A Comparison of Domestic and Foreign Firms in Colombian Manufacturing. 1987. 185 pp. Paper 0-89680-145-4 $10.00.

No. 13   Henderson, James D. Conservative Thought in Latin America: The Ideas of Laureano Gomez. 1988. 229 pp. Paper 0-89680-148-9 $16.00.

No. 16   Alexander, Robert J. Juscelino Kubitschek and the Development of Brazil. 1991. 500 pp., notes, bibliog. Paper 0-89680-163-2 $33.00.

No. 17   Mijeski, Kenneth J., ed. The Nicaraguan Constitution of 1987: English Translation and Commentary. 1991. 355 pp. Paper 0-89680-165-9 $25.00.

No. 18   Finnegan, Pamela. The Tension of Paradox: José Donoso's *The Obscene Bird of Night* as Spiritual Exercises. 1992. 204 pp. Paper 0-89680-169-1 $15.00.

No. 19   Kim, Sung Ho and Thomas W. Walker, eds. Perspectives on War and Peace in Central America. 1992. 155 pp., notes, bibliog. Paper 0-89680-172-1 $17.00.

No. 20   Becker, Marc. Mariátegui and Latin American Marxist Theory. 1993. 239 pp. Paper 0-89680-177-2 $20.00.

No. 21   **Boschetto-Sandoval, Sandra M. and Marcia Phillips McGowan,** eds. Claribel Alegría and Central American Literature. 1994. 233 pp., illus. Paper 0-89680-179-9 $20.00.

No. 22   **Zimmerman, Marc.** Literature and Resistance in Guatemala: Textual Modes and Cultural Politics from El Señor Presidente to Rigoberta Menchú. 1995. 2 volume set 320 + 370 pp., notes, bibliog. Paper 0-89680-183-7 $50.00.

No. 23   **Hey, Jeanne A. K.** Theories of Dependent Foreign Policy: The Case of Ecuador in the 1980s. 1995. 280 pp., map, tables, notes, bibliog., index. paper 0-89680-184-5 $22.00.

No. 24   **Wright, Bruce E.** Theory in the Practice of the Nicaraguan Revolution. 1995. 320 pp., notes, illus., bibliog., index. Paper 0-89680-185-3. $23.00.

Ordering Information

Individuals are encouraged to patronize local bookstores wherever possible. Orders for titles in the Monographs in International Studies may be placed directly through the Ohio University Press, Scott Quadrangle, Athens, Ohio 45701-2979. Individuals should remit payment by check, VISA, or MasterCard.* Those ordering from the United Kingdom, Continental Europe, the Middle East,. and Africa should order through Academic and University Publishers Group, 1 Gower Street, London WC1E, England. Orders from the Pacific Region, Asia, Australia, and New Zealand should be sent to East-West Export Books, c/o the University of Hawaii Press, 2840 Kolowalu Street, Honolulu, Hawaii 96822, USA.

Individuals ordering from outside of the U.S. should remit in U.S. funds to Ohio University Press either by International Money Order or by a check drawn on a U.S. bank.** Most out-of-print titles may be ordered from University Microfilms, Inc., 300 North Zeeb Road, Ann Arbor, Michigan 48106, USA.

Prices are subject to change.

* Please add $3.50 for the first book and $.75 for each additional book for shipping and handling.

** Outside the U.S. please add $4.50 for the first book and $.75 for each additional book.

Ohio University
Center for International Studies

The Ohio University Center for International Studies was established to help create within the university and local communities a greater awareness of the world beyond the United States. Comprising programs in African, Latin American, Southeast Asian, Development and Administrative studies, the Center supports scholarly research, sponsors lectures and colloquia, encourages course development within the university curriculum, and publishes the Monographs in International Studies series with the Ohio University Press. The Center and its programs also offer an interdisciplinary Master of Arts degree in which students may focus on one of the regional or topical concentrations, and may also combine academics with training in career fields such as journalism, business, and language teaching. For undergraduates, major and certificate programs are also available.

For more information, contact the Vice Provost for International Studies, Burson House, Ohio University, Athens, Ohio 45701.